DIGITAL LITERACY

PAUL GILSTER

WILEY COMPUTER PUBLISHING

John Wiley & Sons, Inc.

New York ➤ Chichester ➤ Weinheim ➤ Brisbane ➤ Singapore ➤ Toronto

Copyright © 1997 by Paul Gilster
Published by John Wiley & Sons, Inc.

Library of Congress Cataloging-in-Publication Data:
Gilster, Paul
    Digital literacy / Paul Gilster.
       p.   cm.
    Includes index.
    ISBN 0-471-16520-4 (alk. paper)
    1. Internet (Computer network)   2. Computer literacy. I. Title.
TK5105.875.I57G5297   1997
025.04—dc21   96-46961
                                                      CIP

Printed in the United States of America
10 9 8 7 6 5 4 3 2 1

For Eloise

"So hurry to see your lady,
like a stallion on the track,
or like a falcon swooping down to its papyrus marsh.

Heaven sends down the love of her
as a flame falls in the hay."

—From *Love Songs of the New*
Kingdom (c. 1500–1100 B.C.)

Be not swept off your feet by the vividness of the impression, but say, "impression, wait for me a little. Let me see what you are and what you represent. Let me try you." —Epictetus, *Discourses*

There's nothing so ridiculous but some philosopher has said it. —Cicero, *De divinatione*

Contents

Acknowledgments

Digital Literacy, more than any of my other books, was a collaborative effort. I relied upon the insights and criticisms of numerous people at Wiley, but three deserve special mention. Phil Sutherland was this book's editor. We hammered out its original outline at Internet World in 1995 and over the course of subsequent months wrestled with first this shape, then that, trying all the while to understand the issues driving the astonishing networking revolution that continues to transform all our lives. Phil's energy and perseverance won out, and his insistence that we could uncover underlying truths about the Net helped me to keep the goal in focus. Janice Borzendowski, who I first met as a copy editor on *The Internet Navigator* and who has long since become a trusted friend, helped me to understand the book's strengths and weaknesses; our long conversations, editing and probing over the telephone, provided the intellectual glue that holds these chapters together. Kathryn Malm, who I came to know late in the process, has been a quiet and discerning voice whose reassurances and suggestions have calmed this edgy author on more than one occasion. Thanks, too, to Bob Ipsen for his faith in the concept and willingness to see it through.

Introduction

Like many now caught up by the Internet, I never set
out to be a computer professional. My background is
in the humanities, and before I started doing on-line
research, my technical expertise was minimal. But we
learn by doing, and what I've learned from years of
experience is that the Internet isn't like the places
you and I were trained to understand. If this technology is intimidating, it's because we think in terms of
models that are based on older forms of media. We're
used to television and radio, two ways of communicating that work from the center out. Both call for a
passive approach from their audience; we put ourselves in front of a receiver and absorb the content
offered by networks and local stations. Where the
Internet model diverges is that it places greater
responsibility in the hands of the individual. Rather
than being spectators—information consumers—we
become Internet *users*, people who discover and evaluate content before deciding how to put it to work.

Let me make that last point clearly. It's not hype
to say that the Internet offers something fundamentally different. We've never had the means of connecting so many people with so powerful a set of
tools. Where it all leads is something we are finding
out day by day as the Internet grows and computer

connectivity spreads throughout the globe. But make no mistake about it, this is a different take on communicating, and it calls for a new set of assumptions and a fundamental reorientation in thinking.

No wonder the Internet seems intimidating. You don't just overturn the way people think about the world without causing anxiety. You should realize that your own misgivings about the information revolution are well founded. But your doubts are the strongest asset you bring to the Internet. If this network truly is a revolution in the way we communicate —and it is—then it should stand up to your severest scrutiny. When we look at what troubles people, we can learn truths that otherwise would have eluded us. We'll all understand the Internet better by understanding our misgivings about it. Further, the people who are most active on the Internet today, and who stand to benefit most from its continued expansion, can also learn from our doubts. They're the ones who need to figure out why the Internet is making us restless, challenging our assumptions, overturning our long-held beliefs. They need to know because the Internet will succeed only if it provides real value.

In a sense, we're all experimenting when we use the Internet, because there has never been anything like it before. But the learning curve is not about using an intrinsically difficult technology. Now that the software is easier to use and the hardware is becoming standardized, the real challenge is to rearrange our thinking. Internet content doesn't follow older models, nor does interactive computing let us take a passive approach to information. Content on the Internet is not a static thing. Instead, it is fully interactive. The Internet requires that we understand it as a combination of all the traditional forms of media, and several other forms that change the way we seek out information.

The Internet takes information that would be available in a host of other contexts and gives it three-dimensional shape by linking it to related data. It offers ways to view data in nontextual forms and provides a solution for people who want their information frequently updated to reflect the latest conditions. If we extend these capabilities, it becomes clear that Internet content can be precisely targeted. By using the capabilities of World Wide Web software, we can, for example, save the address of a particularly useful site. The next time we need that information, we just click on the item and go, without having to enter a cumbersome address or work our way back through an entire sequence of Web pages.

Before I became involved with computers, I studied literature and planned to make my living as a writer. I discovered that the Internet was a priceless source of information and contact with the rest of the world, and managed to teach myself how to use it step by step. If I could do that at a time when the Internet was demanding and command-driven, anyone can learn to do it today, when the network is graphically oriented and designed to help the new user. Once you're past the initial hurdles (which are not, in any case, as difficult to surmount as you may think), the Internet will emerge as an inviting community of users. Like any human gathering, it has its quirks, but by hooking into the power of networked computers, you have access to ideas in a way no other medium can offer.

Some people bring unbounded enthusiasm to these issues; they face into the Internet's challenges with a delight in technology and a sure vision of the future. Others, myself among them, approach it as a tool, an access point through which it's possible to reach for information otherwise unavailable, and perform research chores in minutes that supplement and sometimes replace traditional library hunts and scrutiny of bibliographies. And then there are the community builders, who see the Internet as an experiment in democracy, its communication outlets its most precious asset; that these create still further sources for information gathering is yet another beneficial result.

So we needn't see the Net as a single thing; its unique nature is shown by the manifold changes it rings on old themes. I can make it into a platform for the study of antiquity if I choose; on other days, I use it to explore the farthest reaches of the universe. It's a window to the Hubble observatory as well as a discussion area for homeless-shelter directors and a refuge for would-be actors. Nor are its uses necessarily benign. A bogus account of an airline disaster can be propagated as news when a naive journalist finds it on the Net. Misinformation—and disinformation—breeds as easily as creativity in the fever-swamp of personal publishing. Ideologues and self-promoters abound. It will take all the critical skills users can muster to separate truth from fiction.

I see the Internet as a city struggling to be built, its laws only now being formulated, its notions of social order arising out of the needs of its citizens and the demands of their environment. Like any city, the Net has its charlatans and its thieves as well as its poets, engineers, and philosophers. This shouldn't surprise us; we've been facing the same issues of growth, order, and justice since the time of the Sumerians, whose own contribution to the technology of ideas—the inscribed clay tablet—still houses their thoughts 5,000 years later in museums around the world. Technology demands of us, as it did of them, a sense of possibilities, a willingness to adapt our skills to an evocative new medium. And that is the heart of digital literacy. Our experience of the Internet will be determined by how we master its core competencies. They are the design principles that are shaping the electronic city.

CHAPTER 1

Literacy for the Internet Age

Acquiring the tools, which are first and foremost con-
ceptual and issue-oriented, will help you cope with
the network in as fully or lightly engaged a way as
you choose. The tools are intellectual and attainable,
for digital literacy is about mastering ideas, not key-
strokes.

The great physicist Ernest Rutherford, frustrated by
the self-important airs of his peers, once told a colleague that a scientist who couldn't explain his theories to a barmaid didn't really understand them. An
idea, in other words, should correspond to a recognizable reality, explainable to an audience larger than a
handful of specialists. Digital literacy—the ability to
access networked computer resources and use them—
is such a concept. It is necessary knowledge because
the Internet has grown from a scientist's tool to a
worldwide publishing and research medium open to
anyone with a computer and modem.

Digital literacy is the ability to understand and
use information in multiple formats from a wide
range of sources when it is presented via computers.

1

The concept of literacy goes beyond simply being able to read; it has always meant the ability to read with meaning, and to understand. It is the fundamental act of cognition. Digital literacy likewise extends the boundaries of definition. It is cognition of what you see on the computer screen when you use the networked medium. It places demands upon you that were always present, though less visible, in the analog media of newspaper and TV. At the same time, it conjures up a new set of challenges that require you to approach networked computers without preconceptions. Not only must you acquire the skill of finding things, you must also acquire the ability to use these things in your life.

The skills of the digitally literate are becoming as necessary as a driver's license. The Internet is the fastest growing medium in history—like it or not, it will affect you and those around you at home and on the job, from the merging of your television set's images with network data to the emergence of communities of users whose activities will change the shape of commerce and education. The Net's growing universality will create priceless resources for learning and self-advancement. If these won't overwhelm your life overnight, they will change it, subtly, continually, and with irresistible force.

Acquiring digital literacy for Internet use involves mastering a set of core competencies. The most essential of these is the ability to make informed judgments about what you find on-line, for unlike conventional media, much of the Net is unfiltered by editors and open to the contributions of all. This art of critical thinking governs how you use what you find on-line, for with the tools of electronic publishing dispersed globally, the Net is a study in the myriad uses of rhetoric. Forming a balanced assessment by distinguishing between content and its presentation is the key.

Other competencies branch inevitably from your ability to think critically. You will have to target your reading using the model of the electronic word—hypertext and its cousin hypermedia, the linking of the individual noun or phrase to supporting text or other forms of media. Sequential reading is supported by nonlinear jumps to alternative idea caches, with inevitable repercussions for comprehension. The journey through text becomes enriched with choices. Consequently, you need to learn how to assemble this knowledge; that is, build a reliable information horde from diverse sources. You must choose an environment within which to work and customize it with Internet tools.

And because the journey through text is flush with choices, developing search skills is the final core competency; it engages you in strategies for using the rapidly proliferating search engines that can hunt through millions of pages of information as you watch, returning a list of targets for your consideration. With the help of these researchers, you can learn how to learn anew; widen an education, support a career change, join a community of like-minded individuals in pursuit of a hobby or an idea. How to pursue is the ultimate issue. Ungoverned and perhaps ungovernable, the Internet's vast holdings catalyze your thinking only if you master the primary skills of the digitally literate searcher.

Today these skills are an adjunct to our normal lives, for the novelty of networking is a long way from wearing off. But the powerful changes in media now occurring throughout the planet argue for a future in which digital literacy is essential. Internet access has been broadened from the original research laboratories that built it to universities worldwide and now to the modem-using public, a public that is signing up for accounts in the millions. On-line services like CompuServe and America Online are acknowledging the Internet's power through their own gateways to the Net. Cable television companies are developing modems that will let them deliver digital data through the cables that already run into your house, while telephone companies and content providers are merging in an effort to pump everything from movies to video games to educational programming through an Internet-enhanced telephone wire.

Who Is the Internet?

That frenzied activity is occurring because the Internet's growth is logarithmic. Estimates of its size are always problematic, there being no central organization keeping tabs on the network, and because counting users means looking at how many networks are connected to the Internet; the problem with the latter is that a single network might include 100, 1,000, or 10,000 users. That's why estimates you see range far afield; one recent survey found 5.8 million users in the United States, in addition to another 3.9 million who used commercial information services like Compu-Serve or America Online.[1] Another survey took the opposite extreme, finding an overall U.S. audience of 42 million users.[2] Who's right? We don't know, but the lower estimate is probably the most reasonable, as it tends to discount the exaggeration that has characterized so many surveys of the Internet's size and growth.[3] But make no mistake, this is one big network, and its winds are growing to gale force.

Let's assume here that something along the lines of 9 million people in the United States have used either the Internet itself or a commercial information service. We'll then factor in Internet growth, which has seen recent rates of close to 100 percent annually, with some parts of the network, like the World Wide Web, enlarging at an even faster clip.[4] One London-based research firm sees 200 million users worldwide by the year 2002.[5] A new network connects to the Internet every 10 minutes. And perhaps you can get a clear idea of how far electronic networking has already spread by comparing it to a more familiar form of information transfer. Consider then that the number of electronic mail messages the network carried in 1995 outnumbered the number of postal messages delivered by U.S. mail carriers that year.[6]

Who are these people? The great majority of the Net's inhabitants are male, although their percentage seems to be dropping as we move toward broader participation from small businesses and homes. It's a young audience, more than half between the ages of 18 and 34, and it's a relatively affluent audience as well, although more so in the United States than in overseas markets.[7] Two-thirds of the users in one survey have a college degree.[8] But the demographics are in dizzying motion. As the Internet flourishes, its population will more and more resemble that of a typical city, the same audience served by former technological breakthroughs like television and telephone.

The Internet, in short, is showing signs of the kind of breakout that will make it ubiquitous. Network access will become as common as the telephone jack. Will you be ready to use it? Business is moving rapidly to embrace the network paradigm, so you're likely to encounter the Internet face to face in the office even if you don't choose to tap it at home. Corporations are learning how to meld their databases to readily accessed World Wide Web interfaces, and at the same time they are putting the burden on employees to demonstrate literacy in things digital without background or training. The Net's emergence as a mass medium, propelled by huge commercial interests hunting for breakthroughs in global advertising, product delivery, and service fulfillment, means you will likewise be confronted with choices as a consumer. Do you buy from the local retailer or the digitized catalog on the Web? Do you find a lawyer who understands global connectivity or look for a traditionalist, and what's the difference in terms of how each can help you? Do you advertise your own product on the Net, and if so, where's the best location?

The scope of our information glut also demands an Internet-oriented solution. Content has run amok, as scholar and critic Neil Postman noted in a 1990 speech. In that year in the United States, 11,520 newspapers and 11,556 periodicals played a relentless jingle of information and updates, while 362 million television sets and over 400 million radios pounded out the back beat. Out of fully 300,000 new book titles around the globe, 40,000 were published in the United States. In that same year, Americans took 41 million photographs and received over 60 billion pieces of junk mail. They bought videotapes from 27,000 stores and read advertisements from 260,000 billboards. Can anyone doubt that these numbers have undergone a quantum jump since? Their magnitude makes the point as well as anything that learning to manage the multimedia flow and to superimpose network-driven information filters is becoming—if it isn't already—a critical skill.[9]

Digital Convergence: A Collage of Media

Convergence is the word of the hour because networked information opens your desktop to a global data bank, challenging old models of distribution. Radio stations are learning how to feed their programming through the Net, erasing geographical boundaries and changing the meaning of the term *broadcasting*. We learn to use bizarre buzzwords like *pointcasting* and *narrowcasting* to describe such content on demand. Individuals become publishers using easily available tools, while magazines and newspapers wrestle with subscription models in the on-line medium they have embraced out of necessity.

Convergence takes advantage of the fact that data in all its forms—text, video, audio, graphics—can be turned into the language of binary arithmetic for shipment across the Net. The telephone company, newly freed of governmental restraint, can acquire movies and feed them to your home through the networks it is revamping with fiber-optic connections. The cable television company can become a carrier, and thus an Internet provider, offering high-speed access to the Net as well as standard sitcoms and talk shows. A movie studio, hunting for revenues, can create a fusion between itself and the delivery companies that will pipe its latest fare into homes nation-wide. In similar fashion, media go global, creating opportunities in international commerce for hitherto national and local operations. Internet telephony pushes the human voice in fully interactive form through computer links, disrupting existing rate structures and forcing the long-distance carriers to evaluate their future.

These changes will eventually show up on instruments as prosaic as your television, which will take on invigorated life as a potential Internet conduit. Imagine a set-top Internet box fed by a cable or telephone company, perhaps via satellite, that melds the language of computer data with traditional broadcast media. Flick a switch to move between a PBS documentary on the early exploration of Africa and the World Wide Web site that supports it with background documents and photographs. Send electronic mail to its producer. Or perhaps the model will affect you in reverse. From your desktop PC, flick over to the evening news, putting a windowed Dan Rather in real-time motion in the corner of your screen, even as you explore a vividly realized virtual world with your mouse.

If the television and computer will share significant features in the near future, the Internet interface—what you see when you log on to the Net—will emerge as a standard structure for information retrieval. The World Wide Web, the Internet's most vibrant and fastest-growing precinct, uses programs like Netscape or Mosaic to display content, backed with pull-down menus, icons, and a cursor to click information into reality on-screen. Once driven by user-supplied commands, the Internet's graphical face means that using sophisticated functions on-line is within reach of the average citizen. The difference between these interfaces and the old UNIX command system is similar to the difference between MS-DOS and Microsoft Windows, or MS-DOS and a Macintosh; one requires learning a set of commands before you can use it, while the other makes it easy to experiment by choosing from available menu options, provides help functions, and houses its information in a format that is pleasing to the eye. It's no coincidence that the great explosion of interest in the Internet coincided with the development of such tools on the Web. These tools—*browsers*—made the Internet approachable. We see content as an interactive, typeset magazine with multimedia features; developments such as the Java language and virtual reality promise still more inter-active capabilities.

This browser front end is the point of conver-gence between the Internet and all other forms of media. It is the place where we display content in all its digital array, from plain text to moving video to radio-quality sound, and it is becoming so persuasive a medium that it may eventually replace the stan-dard interface—what you see when you turn on your computer—that governs the way we access programs and call up files. Microsoft Windows will take on the look of a Web browser, with connectivity between local machine and external network rendered virtu-ally transparent. The day the network becomes truly invisible is when it achieves universality, and who can doubt that day is coming? Perhaps not in two years, perhaps not in 10, but within the lifetime of me and my children (and I am not, alas, any longer young). The browser may, for all we know, become a television interface one day, as readily equipped to change channels as to hunt down Web pages. Today, this intuitive interface is another powerful driver for the Net's growth, but one that places demands on anyone who wants to use its deceptively simple tools. If the skills to manipulate this readily shaped environment are more approachable than ever, the underlying assumptions aren't. Where will you steer this powerful engine with your newfound point-and-click capabilities? How will you make sense out of what you find?

As the Internet dissolves boundaries like some universal intellectual solvent, we'll all have to understand that what we think we see isn't always what we get. The block-and-tackle equipment of Net publishing is available at low cost and in some cases no cost, depending upon its origin and provenance. The University of London can build a Web page as readily as Hezbollah; the 12-year-old next door can construct a mini-newspaper laden with graphics and typeset-quality text. The anarchy of self-publishing thus confronts the traditional world of branded information—news chosen by editors and exhaustively shaped to fit the vision of a highly regarded publication. What this means is that you must watch your sources on the Internet and learn to sniff out the traits that point to reliability, or you may be sucker-punched by an intellectual charlatan. Advertising likewise becomes deceptively rich; a Web page's sponsors can use content as bait, concealing the underlying pitch. Issues of reliability, conflict of interest, and trust abound.

Navigating these shoals, you'll need to customize your own information feed, requesting daily updates on news tailored to your requirements and accessible through electronic mail or a personalized page on the Web. A personal information strategy, a core competency, includes organizing a wide choice of delivery mechanisms. Call up a newspaper on-line and run keyword searches to find what you need. Receive a personalized newsletter in your mailbox each morning. Create a constantly updating news ticker across your screen. If you choose your data sources right and select out the optimum configuration of topics, you may slip between your competitors and the sun, in classic position for the ensuing dogfight. Choose wrong and your computerized data sweep will tag inconsequential stories, dishing out a vision of the day that falsifies trends and leaves you dangerously complacent. In either case, your life is affected by a series of choices unknown to previous generations, locked in their broadcast model of media. The Internet's power to deliver resources on demand continues to redefine our media.

How publishers cope with the change will measure their future success, too. Some will create a subscription model—pay a set fee for monthly or yearly access, download at will—while others opt for a pay-as-you-go strategy, using the ability of the Internet to charge your credit card for so-called *microtransactions*, a penny per page, a nickel, as determined by the publisher. Pay as you go may also solve the copyright problem, allowing books currently under its protection to appear in digital form, useful for searching and research, even as their printed cousins continue to flourish as the standard vehicle for reading as relaxation and study. The virtual library thus created will be fully searchable on-line, eliminating the library trip, if you know how to tell your browser program to both find and search it. Publishers—and authors—will receive fair compensation, encouraging a continued migration of ideas onto the Net.

The New Geography of Information

In startling clarity, the Internet tugs at your notions of community as well, extending them into the realm of ideas, stretching them across former boundaries. You will be joining discussion groups that encompass people from Tunisia to Brazil, Oregon to Singapore, all communicating through electronic mail, news-groups, and on-line chat. Tuned with scalpel precision to their topics, these clusters of common interest provide support and energy to those in search of an idea or needing help with a problem. Tapping them will increasingly become a part not only of your hobbies but your job description. Communities defined by cyberspace are places where committees go to work on issues at times and places of their own choosing. Consensus develops, a useful process of mutual discussion and analysis that can sharpen a notion into a piercing certainty, or defuse a misconception before it has the chance to blow up in your face. Newly tooled virtual reality software will bring these communities into three-dimensional life on-screen.

Today's worker, whether in a service industry or a factory, increasingly draws on computers for information and process control. The knowledge worker, equipped with the conceptual tools that drive Internet interactivity, becomes mobile, working from home as readily as from the office. The demographic shift this could enable will one day revive rural areas and relieve the congestions of traffic and population density in our cities. Armed with an Internet feed, whether by satellite, telephone jack, or cable modem, the businessperson is encouraged to live where he or she chooses, equally as accessible from the wilds of

New Zealand's South Island as from the power corridors of New York. Those without the necessary mobility become corporate liabilities. The boss wants you in Seattle tomorrow and you'd better be able to access the Net to deliver your report. Can you reach his or her electronic mailbox armed only with laptop and phone jack?

With employment figures problematic and downsizing at our major corporations a fact of life, the security of your current job and the potential of your future endeavors may depend on whether you master these core competencies. The 40-year-old seeking another job may have to think fast in a world governed by instant acquisitions and unexpected layoffs. Acquainting yourself with a quick background in professional issues may mean the difference between success and failure. Discussion groups can do this, as can on-line databases and corporate-sponsored Web pages laced with company and industry resources. Search engines make it possible to conduct the kind of data sweep that makes you, if not an instant expert, at least a player in a fast-changing marketplace.

Employers today frequently post job offerings on the Net, the notion being that those unequipped with the skills to acquire them don't possess the skills to fill the position anyway. Tomorrow's jobs may circulate through network-based job fairs and posting services available only on-line. In any case, arriving at a new employer's office and being confronted with the need to find and evaluate sensitive information puts the burden on you to display shrewdness, insight, and critical judgment, the fodder of digital literacy. The road to advancement, whether in corporate terms or entrepreneurial success, clearly leads Netward, as start-up and Dow 30 company alike are discovering.

Will you be using the Internet—or a form of digital networking that grows out of it—in five years? In ten? Almost certainly. An office worker who masters electronic mail as a way of communicating with suppliers can readily transfer those skills to using e-mail on the Internet. And if you can handle business tasks over a computer network, why not personal chores, like keeping up with relatives in other cities or countries, or asking a group of master gardeners how to grow irises, or learning how to search World Wide Web pages for travel information about Costa Rica? This ready transference of skills from business to home will ensure that the Internet suffuses our lives. For the consumer, finding the right product will increasingly involve a combination of conventional store-hopping and its on-line counterpart. Both fulfill a unique function, the former providing the ability to pick up and judge the item purchased, as well as to socialize and browse in a public setting, the latter offering laserlike search tools to retrieve hard-to-find merchandise the corner mall can't seem to locate for you. Some products translate well to the interactive medium; bookstores are a natural, with their millions of titles, their readily catalogued holdings, and quick delivery via FedEx or UPS. Grocery shopping is a less likely candidate; we want to heft and scrutinize what we'll put in tonight's pasta. Digital skills include knowing when to shop where: When is the on-line store the best choice, and when is it a faddish and unrewarding waste of time?

If these changes are already affecting the lives of many, they are coming full tilt at the lives of the millions still skeptical, unimpressed, or simply averse to technology. The Internet is no more mandatory than a taste for old Bordeaux or a passion for Frescobaldi's harpsichord; the tech police will not impound the lives of the nondigitized. But more often, the dimensions of our daily work and the possibilities of our personal habits will be defined by what we can do in this challenging medium. On that score, acquiring the tools, which are first and foremost conceptual and issue-oriented, will help you cope with the network in as fully or lightly engaged a way as you choose. The tools are intellectual and attainable, for digital literacy is about mastering ideas, not keystrokes.

The Consequences of Technology

Whether we view the Internet as the trigger for a renaissance in the world of ideas or a crisis in the nature of society depends largely upon our preconceptions. A catholic understanding of history implies that it is both, for no technology leaves untouched the people and relationships around it. We should expect to find dislocation in everything from family patterns (you can reawaken communications between long-lost relatives with ease using e-mail, or start a romance through an intriguing on-line chat) to employment security, as new job descriptions bring pressure to bear on more experienced workers. Similarly, we should be open to the positive currents that swirl about this enterprise, to its flexibility in suggesting solutions to long-standing problems, and its inherent power in creating connections between people and institutions where before there were none.

Like television, the Internet is a value-neutral medium; it is a content carrier. Consider the case against TV. It serves up situation comedies that challenge the most sophomoric intellect. Talk shows discuss the private lives of disturbed and disturbing people. Carnage on unprecedented scales enters the home, murders are as routine as weather updates, while the hard sell jabbers from home shopping networks. But *The Man Who Knew Too Much* is there, too, as are *Pride and Prejudice* and *The Abduction from the Seraglio*. No other medium delivers news as it's happening like television, while sports events, stock market analysis, tours of great museums, and Lucy and Desi thrive.

The Internet isn't a package of services or a library of data, though it houses numerous examples of both. It is a conduit. Has it been overhyped? Of course. Yet it is unlikely to be a fad, despite some superficial similarities with short-lived passions like CB radio. Digital networking has established deeper and more significant roots than the average consumer-driven product. For one thing, the Internet works off a proven model of communications that scientists, researchers, and educators have been using in one form or another for over 25 years. That core use, demanding and experimental, has validated the technology. The benefits of connecting computers on a global scale are now being felt on the level of the individual citizen. Few people would describe fax machines or personal computers as fads, because they have become so widely dispersed, essential in workplace and home. As an extension of the personal computer's power, the Internet shows every sign of being as durable—and is conceivably more significant.

Does the Net pose individual and societal dangers? Almost certainly. The history of technology demonstrates convincingly that change on a massive and potentially disruptive scale follows periods of sudden invention. Neil Postman calls technology a Faustian bargain, noting that the tools we absorb in our culture are those that cut a broad swath through previously held beliefs. The printing press opened Europe to powerful currents of dissent, fostered by dogmatists intent on overturning the perceived abuses of the Catholic Church; ironically, its quick adoption by the defenders of Martin Luther played precisely against the hope of its creator, Johannes Gutenberg, that it would serve as a means of spreading Catholic ortho-doxy. Build the printing press and you get individual-ism, dissent, upheaval, a breakdown in the medieval social order. But you also get widespread literacy and a sharp upswing in the notion of democracy.

"Technology giveth and technology taketh away, and not always in equal measure," writes Postman. "A new technology sometimes creates more than it destroys. Sometimes, it destroys more than it creates. But it is never one-sided. . . . Another way of saying this is that a new technology tends to favor some groups of people and harms other groups. Schoolteachers, for example, will, in the long run, probably be made obso-lete by television, as blacksmiths were made obsolete by the automobile, as balladeers were made obsolete by the printing press. Technological change, in other words, always results in winners and losers."[10]

Some of the losers created by the rise of computer networking will be those who allow themselves to become its victims. The image of a frazzled Internet user attached parasitically to his or her computer screen will become as stereotypical as that of the couch potato returning the television's glass gaze, one hand in the tortilla chip bag, the other on the remote con-trol. This is communication as addiction. Among ser-vice providers, it is not uncommon to hear accounts of people who have remained on-line for days at a stretch playing games or engaging in live chat sessions with the similarly enchanted. Michel Landaret, the man responsible for one of France's early chat services, recounts the story of one user who spent 520 hours out of the 720 hours in a month chatting on-line. Another spent 74 consecutive hours at the keyboard.[11]

On-line groups acknowledge the power of the Net to mesmerize; there is even a USENET group called alt.irc.recovery that specializes in helping Internet "addicts" overcome their compulsions. But obsessions run like a radium dye through our social system, from the drug habits of ghettos and Hollywood clubs to the casino fixation of the Las Vegas tourist. Is the Internet symptom or disease? If there is such a thing as an addictive personality, then it's likely that Internet addicts are people who, in the absence of computer networks, would have found some other way to express their compulsions.

Nor are the most lurid accounts representative. A recent study by Nielsen Media Research examined user habits and found that 66 percent of those who said they had logged on in the past 24 hours had done so from work as part of their job; in fact, 30 percent of them didn't own a computer of their own. Their average amount of on-line time was five and a half hours per week, hardly what I would call an addiction.[12] In fact, what the Internet seems to be accomplishing in many homes is to lure users away from another source of electronic addiction—the aforementioned television. Time spent exploring newsgroups or following World Wide Web hyperlinks is often time that would otherwise have been spent watching sitcoms or talk shows. Shifting attention from a passive medium with limited control over content to an interactive medium offering user participation and genuine opportunities for learning isn't what I would call a bad alternative.

But if the Net will invariably spawn tales of the occasional fanatic, it will also create concern for its more innocent victims, as witness the growing sense of outrage over on-line pornography. Here, the Internet's victims are society's victims, for the Net is nothing if not a reflection of the world out of which it sprang. Of the corner newsstand or the living-room PC, which is the more dangerous carrier of sexual materials, and why? If we say the latter, then we deny the fact that nothing comes to the user who does not demand it. Unlike television, we don't just turn on a computer connection to the Internet and find our screen flooded with images; we have to seek those images out and apply relatively sophisticated software techniques to unpack and view them. That said, it is necessary to add that no parent can afford to be sanguine about these things, for children are adaptive creatures and master technology faster than their overseers. But the solution lies within the industry, with products designed to block offensive materials at the user's, or parents', discretion. To note that these tools are not yet fully effective is to say that we are learning to deal with the Internet as we go, but its history suggests we will find optimum ways to edit its content on the local desktop just as we have found ways to use it as a research and communications tool.

Or perhaps the Net's effects are more subtle, and pernicious, than even pornography. Its effect on education—indeed, its effect on how people think—has come under increasing fire from various quarters, primarily in the humanities. Sven Birkerts book *The Gutenberg Elegies*, for example, is a passionate defense of the written, as opposed to the electronic, word. "The earlier historical transition from orality to script—a transition greeted with considerable alarm by Socrates and his followers—changed the rules of intellectual procedure completely," Birkerts writes. "Written texts could be transmitted, studied, and annotated; knowledge could rear itself upon a stable base. And the shift from script to mechanical type and the consequent spread of literacy among the laity is said by many to have made the Enlightenment possible. Yet now it is computers, in one sense the very apotheosis of applied rationality, that are destabilizing the authority of the printed word and returning us, although at a different part of the spiral, to the process orientation that characterized oral cultures." [13]

Birkerts means that whereas print preserves, indeed immobilizes, language, words on a screen are ephemeral, leading to necessary changes in style and meaning. While his concern is largely with hypertext, with its chain of linkages splaying out the linear function of printed text, they resonate across the entire landscape of technological change, from word processor to on-line electronic journal. He sees the network era contributing to everything from what he calls "language erosion" to a flattening of historical perspectives caused by our reliance on databases rather than texts, with damaging side effects in the realm of personal privacy and individuality.

These warnings are apocalyptic. Cassandra-like, Birkerts and his ilk rail against a doom they see as inevitable, yet their prophecies lack the historical context that would reveal them as imprecise and unlikely. The printed word, after all, is the result of a technology, one that allowed the fixation into print of words that were previously handcrafted. The act of writing partakes of a technology, too; the earliest clay tablets fixed the spoken word in tangible fashion on a medium that would preserve it when the syllables that uttered it had long died away. Technology is not merely machinery; it is a fashioning of implements; its Greek root refers to the systematic treatment of an art or craft. The greatest technological shift in the domain of thought was the invention of an alphabet; our papyrus rolls, codices, printing presses, and Internets are but variations on that theme.[14]

But there is another aspect to this discussion that strikes at a more personal level. Clifford Stoll's book *Silicon Snake Oil* is deeply skeptical about the effects of networking on our values. Stoll is an astronomer who has used networks for years and is conversant with their ways. His earlier book, *The Cuckoo's Egg*, is an account of his pursuit of a German hacker who was breaking into computer systems at Berkeley and elsewhere.[15] That battle of wits involved tracing minute evidence on a global network; in a sense, the Internet was the book's hero. But *Silicon Snake Oil* takes an entirely different slant. "By logging on to the networks," Stoll writes, "we lose the ability to enter into spontaneous interactions with real people. Evening time is now spent watching a television or computer terminal—safe havens in which to hide. Sitting around a porch and talking is becoming extinct, as is reading aloud to children." [16] And so on.

Silicon Snake Oil is an engaging book; every Internet user should read it for its necessary reality check. But the notion that computers are replacing human interactions is profoundly wrong. The Internet is nothing if not a powerful communications tool. True, the digital exchange of electronic mail, to cite one example, is in at least one sense impersonal; we'll doubtless never meet the great majority of the people we talk to on the Internet. Offsetting this is the fact that we are exposed to people and cultures we would otherwise never have known. Because my electronic mail address has appeared in all my books, I get messages from all over the globe. I've held discussions and have cultivated friendships using the on-line medium; in many ways, the diversity of this experience has enhanced, not diminished, my ability to relate to the people who are physically near me.

Max Frisch called technology " . . . the knack of so arranging the world that we don't have to experience it."[17] That's a darkly ironic view, but it ignores the fact that technology is likewise something we experience; it is very much a part of our world. In recent times, writers like Kirkpatrick Sale and Bill McKibben have lamented the cultural and physical damage wrought by the Industrial Revolution,[18] thus joining a tradition of technological skepticism that began in the late eighteenth century. Consider Mary Wollstonecraft Shelley, whose nightmarish *Frankenstein* (1818) grows logically into the machine-age dystopias created by science fiction writers like John Brunner and William Gibson. From Thoreau to today's survivalists, technology has always bred unease.

But science continues to produce tools, and we continue to use them. I see the Net as having the same effect all technology does: It offers new possibilities that have to be considered within the context of an unchanging human nature. In that sense, the Internet is as ordinary, and as powerful, as the telephone. Telephones haven't changed our need to talk to other people; what they've provided is a way to do so over distance, so that we can keep in touch with those we love or work with no matter where they live. Both the telephone and the Internet change society; it's much easier for families to move to different places when they can maintain connections through other than physical means. From the cave painters of Lascaux to the pyramid builders of Egypt and the Yucatan to the engineers of Panama and Apollo, history has been one long encounter with the technological flood tide. And because history also suggests that we can't step out of those currents, our challenge is to use technology in ways that enrich the human experience.

CHAPTER

The Nature of Digital Literacy

Whereas traditional media offer *content, the Internet requires you to* build *content from the huge resources it puts at your disposal.*

When in late Roman times books began to appear in codex form, with pages that could be turned rather than unrolled like papyrus, the process of locating information changed. Now the reader could easily move backward in the text to find a previously read passage, or browse between widely separated sections of the same work. With one technological change, cross-referencing became feasible, while the physical space needed to house a collection of books was sharply reduced. Page numbers became a possibility, as did indexes; tables of contents became workable references.[1]

The work of Johannes Gutenberg likewise changed the way people looked at information. The printing press was a dramatically populist invention; it lowered the cost of books by making it possible to mass-produce them. The era of the Gutenberg Bible (1456) became an information age in its own right, a time when radical technologies multiplied at dizzying rates the number of books available to the populace. Forty years after Gutenberg's work was complete, 110 cities in six different countries contained printing presses; ten years after that, the number of printed books totaled 8 million.[2]

Whereas the movement from papyrus and parchment roll to codex made modern library science possible, the quickening impulse of Gutenberg's press took the distribution of ideas into the hitherto unexplored realm of the mass media. With the help of Gutenberg, the average person could hope to build a small library, and ideas could propagate at a faster pace because manuscripts formerly duplicated by hand now moved through an automated production process. Inevitably, this technological change produced cultural crosscurrents. The possibility of meaningful self-education arose. In the universities, students gained access to materials that would otherwise have been laboriously shared. The uncontested sway of the printed word would last 500 years, spurring the development of the Reformation and the Renaissance, before a significant rival technology emerged. And as I will argue later, digital networking supports and extends the power of print rather than supplanting it. The two technologies intertwine like DNA strands, the double helix of the twenty-first century's intellectual revival.

We tend to forget this when coping with the everyday assault of network news; we read about technology as an end in itself. What dominates the headlines is the latest breakthrough in chip design, or the development of software that allows people to talk to computers, or the creation of on-line interactive worlds through virtual reality programs. But beneath all the chatter, routes of communication are being tunneled out in our culture. These routes connect us not only with a digitized future but with the archives of our past.

The Internet is an experiment that explores such connections. It is currently in its adolescence, if not its infancy. And while it has been with us since 1969, it is only within the last few years that the Net has taken on the dimensions of a global community not delimited by geography, professional status, or government affiliation. Thanks to it, we're learning how to navigate through forms of content that once were available only via the broadcast media. We can share that content as readily with other people as we exchange postal letters or telephone calls, through vehicles such as electronic mail, interactive chat, and multimedia pages on the World Wide Web. Much as the invention of a phonetic alphabet made it possible to transform an existing medium (speech) into an elastic new form (the written word), so the Internet transforms the ways we share ideas. Its evolution parallels that of a biological ecosystem, an ever changing but self-reinforcing environment in which ideas circulate like living organisms, finding their own level, existing with and sometimes being co-opted by competing organisms in the knowledge chain.[3] There is no reason to assume that Darwin's laws don't apply here.

A global web of communications also points to a viruslike spread of ideas. Thus the work of Richard Dawkins: If a genetic pattern is replicated by propagating itself through the reproduction of living things, so ideas are replicated by being passed along from one person to another. Dawkins calls these idea patterns *memes*. "When you plant a fertile meme in my mind, you literally parasitize my brain, turning it into a vehicle for the meme's propagation in just the way that a virus may parasitize the genetic mechanism of a host cell," Dawkins writes. "And this isn't just a way of talking—the meme for, say, 'belief in life after death' is actually realized physically, millions of times over, as a structure in the nervous systems of people all over the world."[4] In Dawkins' terms, the Internet can be seen as a carrier of information on both literal and metaphorical levels; a meme acts much like an infection in being communicated and rapidly spread through a living network, even if that network is silicon- rather than carbon-based.

Digital literacy involves acquiring the necessary survival skills, the core competencies discussed in Chapter 1, to take advantage of this environment. Understanding it requires us to place the Internet within the context of the forms of media that surround it, for a change in the nature of information distribution is once again afoot. We move into an era that blends the all-inclusive concept of broadcasting with the tightly focused world of push-pull, retrieving data on demand.

But what exactly is the digital literacy envelope that encompasses these competencies? We know what *literacy* means; it stands for the ability to use language in its written form. A literate person can read and write his or her native language.[5] In contrast, although computers work with their own languages, such as Pascal and C ++ , digital literacy doesn't mean we have to become programmers or learn to puzzle out long lines of computer code. It refers to a way of reading and understanding information that differs from what we do when we sit down to read a book or a newspaper. The differences are inherent in the medium itself, and digital literacy involves mastering them.

The Internet is an interactive place. It provides content that isn't static—documents, images, sounds, and files are in constant turnover at a given site. A Web page can be updated daily, even hourly; it can be responsive to comments from its users and can provide them with areas in which to chat. Your pathway through its passages is determined by your mouse click, making your experience of hypertext a malleable and personalized phenomenon. Digital information is easily transferable: You can ship a magazine article or a novel around the globe in seconds. You can make one copy of something into two, and send the second to someone else who can, if he or she chooses, duplicate it again. This ability to create clones makes the transfer of information more likely to occur than if you had to resort to a copy machine and the postal service to move the same file; the mechanics of distribution become transparent.

Digital things are also mutable—they can take on any shape as they emerge from the binary soup, so that the Internet's sophisticated routing computers can move my voice as well as my image, and can connect both to the document I place on the World Wide Web. That document contains whatever formatting (design) I choose to give it and relies upon media types that encompass the same spectrum of content as television, radio, and print, only now they can be linked seamlessly so that moving from one to another is effortless. Reduced into the relentless logic of binary arithmetic, its 1s and 0s defining its ultimate decoding into usable content, the Internet's traffic flows, billions of bits per day, over conduits defined by the computers that route its unceasing conversation.

Thus the universe of Internet users is accustomed to a closer proximity in cyberspace than they could ever have achieved in the world of postal mail and telephone calls. I may not know you as anything but an electronic mail address, but if you have sent me a query in the past and I run into something I think would answer your question, I will probably send it to you, or at least send you a pointer to the information's location on the Internet. I do this out of the kind of electronically enabled altruism that the Net has always promoted; by making altruism easier, it is more likely that we will practice it. Indeed, a prime source of information on the Internet is the willingness of Internet users to share resources, as witness the thousands upon thousands of newsgroups in which subscribers discuss issues of interest to them and help each other with problems. The fact that some of these newsgroups are laden with irrelevant or frivolous postings doesn't change the equation: The more Internet users there are, the more likely you are to find answers to your questions on-line, assuming you can learn the skills necessary to ask them. Again, my premise: These skills are more a matter of concepts than keystrokes.

Why do people so frequently respond to electronic mail when they won't answer postal letters or telephone calls? The same person with whom you play telephone tag for days while trying to set up an interview may respond within the hour to an electronic mail message. Sociologists are already writing books about why we do these things,[6] but the practical benefit is obvious: You contact the person you need to speak to, and the needed work gets done. Perhaps it's the sense of participating in an adventure that impels people to behave this way. Especially among those new to the Internet, using electronic mail is a novel, fascinating, and almost addictive experience.

The novelty will eventually pass, as they all do, but it's safe to say that with only a fraction of the world's population able to use computer networks—half the people on earth have no access to a telephone, much less a computer and modem—the sense of community that people find on-line will continue to expand. The Internet's ethic of cooperation accounts for some of its finest sites, and while we're moving to a more explicitly commercial model as the network grows, the willingness to share knowledge persists. You won't find that in many other communications media (a remarkable exception is amateur radio), and it's part of the Internet experience that changes how we think about acquiring information.

So literacy in the digital age—digital literacy—is partly about awareness of other people and our expanded ability to contact them to discuss issues and get help. But it is also an awareness of the way the Internet blends older forms of communication to create a different kind of content. When a company that makes content, like Disney, becomes involved with a company that moves content to people, like Capitol Cities/ABC, you begin to realize that the term *digital convergence* has teeth—sharp teeth. It's what happens when you take things from the analog world of print and radio receiver and translate them into digital bits, the raw stuff that makes computers work. Again I stress that the great realization of the digital era is that *any* form of content can be digitized. We used to think it remarkable that a 10MB hard disk could hold thousands of pages of text, which previously would have occupied multiple filing cabinets in an office.

Today's gigabyte-size hard disk can hold not just text files by the millions, but sound, pictures, and moving video. If you can see it on a television screen, it can be digitized. If you can hear it on a CD player, it can be digitized. If you can think it, it can be digitized.

Digitizing content may sound like the key to multimedia, that great buzzword of the computer era, but in reality multimedia is more than handsomely packaged content. The Internet takes multimedia and networks it, housing linkages between various kinds of information, so that you can move between content sites with ease and incorporate what you find there in your work. Networked multimedia also includes the concept that you are not just reader but participant, involved in the resources you find; you should be able not only to track down the information, but to share it, to add your own thoughts, to incorporate it into your own perspective, to forge links between it and other network sites of a similar nature. The computer is the platform on which this happens; its digital processing kick-starts multimedia, putting mind-amplifying tools enjoyed by no previous generation at your service.

Using this dynamic form of multimedia also requires the ability to find information no matter where it's located. The dilemma we have created by building a global computer network is that we have created a vast information space without a catalog or a directory. The technological answer to this challenge has not been to produce that catalog or directory but to create numerous search tools that let us roam the Internet looking for the content we specify. Consequently, search engines don't resemble library catalogs, just as the Internet itself doesn't resemble any conventional library. A good search engine leverages the power of technology to provide keyword searching across millions of documents, examining their full text to locate your search term and return its address. Such an engine also removes the navigation obstacle by providing a direct link between you and the discovered data. Using these tools within the context of mixed digital content can help you build an education or change a career.

Thus we return to the definition of *digital literacy*: the ability to understand and use information in multiple formats from a wide range of sources when it is presented via computers. A digital read on literacy also involves being able to understand a problem and develop a set of questions that will solve that information need. The problem will be solved using search methods that allow you to access information sources on the Internet and evaluate them. The hypertext experience will show you how reading can be a tightly focused experience, following links to user-determined destinations. The resources thus identified must be then consolidated into a broader package of information that you have gathered from a variety of media sources; the Internet should be considered one among many sources of ideas in a technological society.[7] Combining them, you create an information cache that accesses the processing power of networked computers to provide you with a personalized news environment. Armed with such tools, you are equipped to hunt out ideas for anything from personal interests to professional advancement.

Developing the habit of critical thinking and using network tools to reinforce it is the most significant of the network's core competencies. Master it and the other skills will fall into place. Ignore it and the Internet will remain a dangerous and deceptive landscape. Remarkably for so diverse an operation, the Internet's greatest strength is that it can become what you need it to be. Never has an information facility been so customizable. World Wide Web browsers enable you to compile lists of your favorite sites for quick returns to their pages without entering addressing information. Search engines can be tailored to look for specific keywords and, in some cases, can remember your searches through personal profiles, useful when you want to repeat the search through more recent material. Mailing lists and newsgroups can be chosen that exactly fit your interests, while electronic mail software can be set up with filters to screen out messages from particular senders or ones that contain text on subjects that don't interest you.

Digital literacy is emphatically twin-edged. The Internet provides us with new capabilities for using older media, but it also *creates* content, and that content is interactive and demanding. To look at only one side of this picture is to misjudge what the Net can do. People who are frustrated by the Internet expect it to correspond more closely to the analog world. They see that they can look at newspapers and magazines on-line as well as at the newsstand, but they aren't conversant with how the medium alters the experience of using those resources. Their frustration is exacerbated by the fact that many content providers have also misjudged the medium. Too many magazine sites, for example, parrot the printed edition, without understanding the Internet's ability to broaden the reading experience by incorporating moving video, hyperlinks to archival information, sound clips, discussion areas, supporting databases, and related software.[8]

Digital literacy forces an acquaintance with these facts along with an ability to appreciate the twin nature of the Internet. It is about learning how to back up traditional forms of content with networked, problem-solving tools. But literacy goes beyond developing the skills necessary to use them. Digital literacy is likewise about context. The Internet is, among other things, a publishing medium, one that allows anyone to publish at low cost. It will not cost you more when using your Internet account to participate in a discussion that can be seen by like-minded people around the world. You can join in mailing lists that focus on topics of interest or publish your thoughts in an on-line newsletter. If you're willing to spend more, a World Wide Web page can be a multimedia publishing vehicle that not only allows you to present your ideas, but also lets you set up links to other Web sites, and hence to computers wherever they're located on the network. The sense of geographical limitation rapidly disappears.

All of this has profound implications for how we view what we find on the Internet. Key issues include how we evaluate content and make decisions based on what we've found. In a world where anyone can publish, are all publications suspect? On a network where the basic tools of publishing are in many cases free, is it too easy to produce deceptively sophisticated content? Are there dangers in misleading people into thinking they're dealing with experts when they might be dealing with cranks?

These are troubling questions that deserve better answers than they have received. The Net is a publishing medium in the most democratic sense. What it will grow into should be the subject of a great national debate. What it is today is something between what media hype would have you believe and what detractors would have you reject. Today's Internet rookies can have a material effect on how it evolves by becoming network participants themselves—thus the notion of the Internet as a kind of ecosystem. The balance of nature in a healthy ecosystem is maintained by countless factors at work within the environment to produce stability. Each node on the Internet network exists in the same kind of relationship to the broader ecosystem of cyberspace. Common protocols allow different kinds of computers to transmit and receive data. No one computer site makes decisions for the entire network, just as no one lake or stretch of forest determines what happens to the environment that sustains it. An ecosystem maintains itself in the face of adversity; trees grow back after forest fires, crops grow again after floods. The Internet maintains itself through its robust protocols. If a computer goes down, data reroutes itself to reach its destination. If the network becomes congested with traffic, the message flow slows, but the network keeps working.

It's a malleable thing, this Internet. There being no fixed center to the network, the choices you make, from the selection of a service provider to the kinds of content you decide to call up on-screen, are entirely in your hands. The Internet can be a news engine, a financial-market assistant, a mail carrier, a catalog, or an encyclopedia. It can be a research database or a gameplayer. It can provide access to these things and more through software programs specifically designed to mine their various features. The key precept in all of this is user choice, and that involves a key reversal of traditional roles.

The Great Paradigm Shift

If the overarching core competency of Internet use is critical thinking, to explain its application on-line we must move beyond the concepts we have been taught to apply to other media. The Net refuses to mimic other forms of media in most important respects. These media are just learning how to adapt to the Internet, and while numerous experiments are in motion, few companies or content providers of any stripe have figured out the best way to transform their material into digital format. Try to read a newspaper on-screen in the traditional way—page by page, ad by ad—and you'll find yourself asking why your eyes become so fatigued, or why the Internet lacks the easy accessibility of a printed newspaper. The same holds true with books. Who wants to read an entire book on-line, even if it's readily available? What good is it, considering you can buy the same book at the local bookstore, page back and forth within it easily, and read it without eyestrain while enjoying a glass of wine by the fireplace?

This question is a barrier you must punch through. The Net changes the relationship between content provider and audience. Such shifts in perspective are disruptive, certainly; recall the galvanic swings in thinking and research that followed the work of Copernicus, of Newton, of Einstein. By altering the way humans conceive of the universe, these thinkers changed forever the methodology of science. Remarkably, each also built upon the others; Newtonian physics works in a sun-centered solar system, and it will get you to the outer planets, but Einsteinian relativity is what it takes to understand the light from distant suns. The work of each of these men caused a rift in an accepted view, inevitably controversial because it reflected upon previous theories and challenged the beliefs of scientists who based their understanding upon the old system.

In a similar way, the Internet and its accompanying blitz of technological transformation pushes up against a media model we have long accepted. It forces a shift in paradigms that will make you reevaluate older ways of information gathering even as you learn to incorporate them into the new. The Internet is not a gradual shift in the way we work. Instead, it is an analog-to-digital transformation that will alter the rules of communication.

Transformation is best described by contrast. Think about the assumptions you make when you sit down in front of the television. Even with the advent of cable and the expanding number of channels, television places limits on content. You know when you flick on your set, for example, that while violence is tolerated on crime shows, it won't be of the graphical sort that shows up on many first-run movies. The film on network television is often prefaced by a notice that its content has been edited. Extreme violence is one thing it's edited for; sexual content is another. The executives in charge of programming have made decisions that act as a filter that determines what we see.

In that sense, television is an *exclusive* medium— it excludes certain categories of content from distribution. The economics of these limitations are obvious. Television stations have to be careful about offending too many people, for fear they will lose their advertisers. They function through a broadcast model—the same signal goes out to all viewers—and that means that since a given station can reach everyone with its content, a consensual approach to that content is mandatory. The principle is to offend as few people as possible while appealing to a broad, popular taste.

The Internet operates by a different set of rules; it is an *inclusive* medium. No central organization determines what goes onto the Internet, nor is there any sense of accountability to a mass audience. Indeed, in a significant sense, there is no mass audience. Rather than distributing content indiscriminately, the Internet works by offering options; you could think of it as a television with millions of channels, each of which contains an interactive element that lets you chart your own course in exploring its resources. You use search tools to find which of these "channels," or sites, best fit your own set of interests. And the people who make the content available— individuals, organizations, companies, clubs, governments—hope to provide specific information that will lure you to their sites. True, there is no Internet "programming" in the television sense. But there is content that is designed to attract users who have a particular information need. And just as television broadcasts *out*, the Internet draws users *in*.

The Power of the Networked Computer

The paradigm shift in content reflects immense changes in the nature of computing. The desktop computer revolution—and the networking of machines that transformed it—has transferred some of the functionality of computing out of the hands of specialists and into the machines, and minds, of everyday users. The calculations that once could be run only by the technically proficient are now easy to perform using off-the-shelf software. Local area networks connect office workers to powerful corporate information banks. The Internet itself has moved from a government-sponsored experiment used by researchers and academics to a broadly based information tool that can be tapped by anyone with a computer and modem or a dedicated connection in the workplace.

All of this trades upon the power of connected computers. The stand-alone computer on a desktop can run thousands of programs from its own hard disk, but if we link that computer to a second one, so that the two can share information, we expand its capabilities not only in terms of access to more computer files, but also in terms of communications. To link two computers is to build a digital bridge; it allows us to reach the person who operates the second computer in a surprisingly productive way. Because computers store information, we can send messages that stay on the other computer's hard disk until they are read. We can exchange interesting files—text or data—with the other user, or swap programs that can run on either machine. We can use one computer to manipulate data on the other, extending the power of both and sharing the result.

Our two linked computers exist as equal members of a simple network. Networks are formed when computers—not terminals—are linked. And because each of our two computers houses its own processor, neither of them can be said to be in charge of the operation. If I am linked to your computer, I can send you files and you can send me messages, but neither of us has made our machine subservient to the other's.

Here the paradigm shift becomes obvious. When you watch television, you turn a switch and view what the various channels show you. When you participate in a rudimentary network like the one we've just created, the process becomes active. Unless you or the person at the other end of the connection does something, nothing will happen. Whereas traditional media *offer* content, the Internet requires you to *build* content from the huge resources it puts at your disposal. The content available is a consequence of the way the network itself operates; because it has empowered individuals to use digital means to publish information, the Internet offers access to a veritable data bazaar.

We can see this principle more clearly if we extend our basic network. We started by connecting two computers together, but there is no rule that says a network must consist of only two connected machines. If we continue connecting computers, building a larger and larger network, we can create an environment where it's possible to speak of a *user community*, a collection of individuals who can exchange information, from messages to data files, among themselves. And we can go a step beyond this model as well. One computer network, set up, for example, at a business office or the headquarters of an organization, can in turn be linked to another computer network. The scale of the Internet becomes apparent when you realize that it consists of tens of thousands of these networks. And each of them can contain hundreds or thousands of users.

One of the great figures in computing is Bob Metcalfe, who invented the networking scheme called Ethernet, which is a way of connecting computers that made networks practical in the business office.

Metcalfe's law is a way of describing what happens to the power of a computer when you link it to other machines. The law states that for any number n of computers, their performance and value increase by a factor of n squared when you connect them. Put 4 computers onto a network, in other words, and you wind up with the equivalent power and functionality of 16 machines, thus taking maximum advantage of your resources. Now imagine linking millions of machines into a global Internet. What new capabilities are being created?

The power of the Internet comes from the fact that these connections are decentralized. No one of these machines, no cluster of networks, can be said to run the enterprise. Democracy prevails: I can publish a message on the Internet as readily as you. I can choose which topics to read about and switch off those that don't interest me. I can navigate the information space by making choices, running searches for keywords, and displaying content. Depending on my interests, I can become a content provider or remain a reader, meaning that what I get out of the Internet is very much a matter of personal preference. No one other than myself makes the choices about what I see.

The beauty of this is that no one is asking you to give up other sources of information just to use the Internet. In its broadest sense, the Internet exists as one of a choice of media now making available to us the greatest amount of information ever accessible by individuals. Peter Large estimates that more new information was created in the past 30 years than had appeared in the previous 5,000.[9] More and more, this information is appearing through the medium of networked communications, but it can be supplemented by the tools that are familiar to you, the televisions, radios, and newspapers that form so much a part of our daily lives. The information choices we make and our judgments of what we see and read are determined by a mixture of all these sources. But increasingly, the Internet will play a role in defining the possibilities.

This also explains why the Internet can sometimes seem a demanding place, so laden with information that we barely know where to begin. In a real sense, the Internet is a reflection of society at large, one that is becoming a more accurate mirror than any other form of media. By removing the information filters that govern what we read and see, the Net gives us a kind of choice over our information that is unique in the history of communications. When it puts the new tools of digital publishing in the hands of the average user, the Internet rounds out the massive redistribution of ideas that began with Gutenberg's printing press. It also provides a sizable boost to libertarian democracy.

A Changing Model of Access

The Internet was never conceived as a searchable archive, much less a publishing tool for individuals, when it took shape in the 1970s with funding from the Department of Defense. Its growth in the 1980s, backed by the National Science Foundation, was largely in the universities, connecting them with the supercomputer sites that housed the world's most powerful machines. But communications creates relationships; ideas cluster, flourish, and spawn new research. Soon academics were talking by electronic mail, then exchanging professional news through mailing lists. Taking the Net into the commercial arena was a development of the 1990s, but this third wave of expansion has transformed it from a specialist's resource to a society-changing communications carrier.

The Internet has traditionally been a sharing place, where the power of ideas takes precedence. Now it has also become a place where ideas generate revenues. The commercial growth of the network has seen the development of numerous software tools to support Web access and improve browser design. Today, business considerations are driving prices lower while setting into motion fierce competition between companies looking to position themselves in cyberspace. Like the wide-open Internet of the early years, today's network remains responsive to the free flow of information even if it now occurs in a market environment that is evolving its own mechanisms of network access.

The commercial Internet is the one you have seen blitzed across newsmagazines, television shows, and newspaper headlines. For the individual user, the commercial model means this: You must choose among payment plans for your access, and locate your own best route to go on-line. This means you will pay a monthly charge, anywhere from $20 to $35, to an Internet service provider (ISP). The service provider is a company that offers Internet access to individuals and companies. It buys access in large quantities from network providers and sells that access individually to its customers.

Notice how decentralized this model is. The Internet has been adding networks since the 1970s, each of which has been responsible for the issues surrounding its own connection. Absent federal funding, there is no central access point, no main office, no 800 number to call for the Internet at large. When you sign on, your modem connects you to a local telephone number, even if the provider you use is based in another city. Your provider—it could be as large as a national long-distance carrier or as small as a two-person office in your hometown—offers to sell you access for a price that it, not the Internet at large, determines. Market forces dictate how that price fluctuates.

All of which can be confusing for those who visualize the Internet in the same terms they apply to commercial information services like CompuServe or America Online. These information companies run extensive advertising campaigns, so that the image of people using computers with modems is often associated with their names. And to further complicate matters, they and their competitors have begun moving into the Internet arena, recognizing that interest in the Net isn't going to lessen. Through their own gateways to the Internet, they position themselves as Internet service providers in their own right. So what are the real differences between them and the Internet at large?

The commercial services, unlike the Internet, are centralized businesses operating off a hub of primary computers. CompuServe, for example, maintains its headquarters in Columbus, Ohio, where it runs network operations on its mainframe computers. When you place a call to a local access number, your data is ultimately routed through the Columbus site. This centralization likewise means that account information is established and maintained at a single source, which you can query when you have questions and count on for updates. America Online and Prodigy have adopted similar models, although with their own software user interfaces. By charging per-minute fees, they have garnered subscribers by offering content available only on their services. With their separate, proprietary networks, the commercial information services have followed a model that is directly challenged by the growth of the Internet. If an Internet service provider offers unlimited access at a flat rate, the user compares that to the by-the-minute charges the on-line information services have traditionally billed and realizes that the ISP offers the better deal, assuming more than a few hours of on-line time per month. In that case, why not just go to an Internet provider and forget the commercial information service altogether? The question isn't an idle one, for the explosive growth of the Internet has led to a proliferation of freely available content that in many ways competes with what the CompuServes and America Onlines offer for a fee.

Their response to the challenge is twofold. First, they point to proprietary materials. CompuServe, for example, maintains a series of full-text databases that are useful in research. One database is made up of general-interest magazines, another of computer periodicals, still another of health-related journals. A CompuServe user can search these materials by keyword and pay an additional fee determined by the number of articles retrieved. Without a CompuServe account, those databases are unavailable to the Internet user (or available only through other services that likewise charge by the article).

Forums are another case in point. A CompuServe forum is a discussion area, moderated, usually, by volunteers and divided into sections according to the subject. Thus a forum on wine might be divided into sections according to the various growing areas; users would be able to ask questions of other wine enthusiasts or compare tasting notes about their favorite vintages. These forums, like the databases, are available only to members, as are the company's news services, chat areas, and a host of other materials.

By offering this proprietary content, the commercial information services hope to maintain and expand their customer base by emphasizing their Internet-access capabilities. DELPHI was the first commercial information service to provide Internet access to its members, offering electronic mail, file transfer, and other Internet options through a character-based interface. The other commercial services began to follow suit, starting with electronic mail and gradually extending their reach.

The growth of the World Wide Web has now led all of them to find ways to tie their proprietary software packages into the Internet. CompuServe and America Online have made arrangements with Microsoft and Netscape to make their browser software available to users who want to explore the Web; CompuServe has even announced that it will phase out its proprietary software entirely in favor of Web-based delivery. The commercial services are also dropping their prices; the new model is to offer cost-efficient access on a monthly basis, often through some sort of flat-rate plan. Unlimited use for $19.95 seems to be the new price point. These companies know they are in a war for survival, but they count on their relative ease of use and comparatively robust on-line support to keep them viable.

As the commercial services begin to close the distance between themselves and the Internet, their offerings should increasingly mirror what Internet service providers sell, although there remain questions about access speed and price. Anyone using a commercial service on a by-the-minute basis will quickly regret the choice if the goal is heavy Internet use, as the price will soon escalate beyond control. But flat-rate plans will test whether the commercial services' customers value the sense of community present in the proprietary service or the broader route to the Internet made available by an Internet service provider. One thing is for sure: No user will lack for access options.

On the Internet, access is a gateway to content, but it is also a window on diversity and change. The Net's growth has been particularly concentrated in World Wide Web sites, each of which can be considered a publishing venture in its own right, whether as a front end for a company's catalog, an electronic newsletter for hobbyists, or a personalized presentation of world news. With growth rates running between 50 and 100 percent per year, the Web and its on-line archive continues to swell with data, most of it searchable and available for reading or download. What you see on the Internet today is a subset of what you will see tomorrow. Each day begins the hunt anew.

CHAPTER

An Internet Day

High technology and daily life mix intriguingly on today's Internet, a welcome outcome of the Net's great democratization.

No two Internet days are alike, for the Net's pathways are as divergent as the route variations on a detailed road map. What you can do and where you can go on the Internet from the same starting point each morning will vary every time you click a different hyperlink to an unknown destination and, having explored that site, move from there to another. The Web page you choose as your home base is where your browser launches each day's journey, but it is nothing more than a base camp before a wild and untamable Everest.

My own journeys begin early. I'm in the office well before 8:00, a second cup of coffee by the keyboard, my Border Collie snoozing on her dog bed beside the desk; on the muted television, a scrolling ticker tape shows yesterday's closing stock prices, while the radio plays Telemann. I've double-clicked the Internet icon and my software is dialing the phone; I can hear dial tone and then the digital beeping of number entry. Entering my user ID and password, I see the system hesitate, then recognize me, launching the unreadable data stream that tells me I'm locking onto the worldwide cyberflow. The Internet protocols negotiate with my service provider's computer for an address to attach to my machine; finding one, they carry me onto the Net as if down a tidal river. Netscape, my World Wide Web browser, appears on-screen, its icon in the pulsing dance that tells me it is making the connection that will display data. And soon the data comes, painting images on the screen, a welcome from my Internet gateway.

As a modem user, I'm not assigned a static Internet Protocol (IP) address. Instead, my provider assigns addresses on the fly—I receive whichever address happens to be next in queue. The process takes place behind the scenes. From my perspective, as my strategy for the day slowly crystallizes, I see only what is taking shape on the screen. After the first cacophonous sounds from the modem, I'm looking at the World Wide Web, which for all intents and purposes has become my Internet environment. Like any other program, it exists in a window on my desk. With one click, I can expand it; with another, I can iconize the global network, moving seamlessly between it and my word processor, daily scheduler, or electronic mail program.

At full-screen size, the Web page is attractive, its various textual items highlighted in blue and underlined to advise me they are hyperlinks—click on any one of them and I will be taken somewhere else. It might be to another file on the same computer, or it might be to an image on a computer halfway around the world. All this works through an underlying language called HyperText Markup Language (HTML) that drives the World Wide Web. Each image, each header, corresponds to an HTML setting inserted with a jeweler's precision by the programmer who created this Web page.

Grouping the News

Today I want to start by catching up on my research in the newsgroups. If I let my newsgroups go unread for long, I'll ultimately become overwhelmed, hundreds of postings waiting in queue and only so many hours in the day to read them. The result: I treat them like unread newspapers, discarding them en masse. I don't want that to happen, so I minimize Netscape and call up my newsreader software, a separate program whose sole function is to examine the newsgroups to which I subscribe, downloading messages that have accumulated during my absence from the network.

It's a beautiful morning outside. I take another sip of Kenya AA and watch a hawk wheeling across the sky, out early in search of breakfast. I think about how the Internet has changed the very concept of news. Certainly, it's not news that hawks circle in the sky, but if someone writes a reflection about hawks and hunting and posts it on an Internet newsgroup called rec.arts.writing, it becomes news. That newsgroup is a discussion area, a place where people who write things go to exchange ideas, swap gossip about editors and markets, and learn about each other's work. It's also news when someone adds to the ongoing discussion, contributing an insight that everyone can see, and prompting responses from still other subscribers who will remember that day, that message, and that hawk, and maybe write something new because of all these things.

On-screen, my software, called Agent, has found the news server, the computer that manages the newsgroup traffic at my provider's site. Having located it, Agent is synchronizing the message traffic, matching the messages on the server with what it knows about which groups I'm subscribed to and which messages within those groups I've already read. I could read the new messages now, but I have other things in mind. It has been a long time since I downloaded the entire list of newsgroups from the server; this is a useful exercise, as it brings me up to speed with any recently added newsgroups.

Soon, I've downloaded a revised list from my service provider. The list totals some 14,000 newsgroups, although this is actually a subset of the total number available throughout the Internet. After all, newsgroups are easy to create. Anyone with an idea can check to see if the topic is already covered, and if not, there are various ways to establish a new group. With group creation happening all over the globe, it's easy to see that my local provider may not carry them all. Besides, some are unabashedly local, covering topics of interest to people in a particular country or region.

I can page through the list of newsgroups if I choose or use Agent's search function to target particular ideas. This morning I decide to move around the list at random. Here's alt.sports.football.pro.miami-dolphins. Phew! That's some moniker. The newsgroup hierarchical name structure can make a topic blindingly clear, but these names don't exactly roll trippingly off the tongue. How about misc.writing. screenplays? Probably a good place to be if I'm thinking about a career move to Hollywood, but I've got my hands full right here in North Carolina. Paging down the list, I find news.announce.newusers, a helpful starting point for novices to the newsgroups. Here's sci.psychology.theory, as opposed to the more practically oriented sci.psychology.research, or the intriguing sci.psychology.consciousness. Here's talk.politics .china and misc.jobs.offered. And some harder news, via clari.biz.economy or clari.biz.finance. The latter give me wire-service updates about the topic in their titles.

The problem is obvious. Which do I read? I often build a list of newsgroups that I intend to follow religiously, but when I sign on the next day, I find I've subscribed to too many. The list of waiting messages overwhelms me, and I must resign from several until I have established a number I can manage. Unlike magazine subscriptions, the newsgroups are areas you move into and out of, experimenting to find the ones that best suit your schedule and your interests. That makes a good newsreader essential.

USENET, the communications tool that became the newsgroup phenomenon, used to be separate from the Internet; its messages traveled using their own methods, connecting UNIX-based computers on a national and then global basis. But today, most USENET traffic is readily available over the Internet, with each service provider making the call as to which groups to carry. Usually, a provider will carry the big groupings that cluster under names like comp, talk, misc, and so on. These give you a broad-brush characterization of their subgroupings. Thus, alt stands for alternative, a younger and looser collection of groups than some of the others; misc stands for miscellaneous, where the loose ends fit. The comp hierarchy is where the computer groups find their niche, while the talk groups hold lively debates about controversial subjects. The list goes on; there's a rec hierarchy for recreational topics like waterskiing and stamp collecting, a biz group for business subjects, and so on. Each of the hierarchies is broken into progressively finer-grained subcategories, until we arrive at the level of the individual newsgroup, which could be anything from the relatively straightforward sci.classics to the tongue-twisting alt.business.import-export.raw-material.

My newsreader checks the messages in each group I'm subscribed to whenever I log on with it; it then groups those messages by *thread*, which is another way of saying that it arranges the messages so that every message on a particular subject is followed by the next message on that subject, and so on. A good newsreader is indispensable; it's your newsgroup information manager, and you'll learn its moves until they're instinctive.

Like most other forms of Internet activity, the newsgroups are becoming multimedia in their own way. They weren't designed to be such, but the impulse toward media mixing increasingly defines the Internet. I can't get that hawk out of my mind, so I cut over to a newsgroup called alt.binaries. pictures.animals. I'm scouting for a photo that, once located, I can download and display. My newsreader will take the coded text file of that photograph and perform its magic, rendering it into an image that I can feed to my graphics viewer. I find no hawk this day, but I do find a condor, soaring over the Andes: a lovely, full-color photograph someone has thought to share by posting its image on a newsgroup read by people who enjoy nature photography and the glories of the wild.

Back to business, I run through my regularly subscribed newsgroups, letting my newsreader tell me how many new messages are in each one. In alt.wired, 109 show up. This is the newsgroup in which readers of *Wired Magazine* regularly talk about cyberspace issues. That's a lot of messages, but they're shown by subject line, grouped into threads. I can choose the subjects that sound interesting, and Agent always alerts me to the presence of new messages in the topics I've been regularly following. I breeze through alt.wired on high octane, snaring three threads, saving a message from one for insertion into my local archive.

Next is alt.internet.culture, with 42 postings about issues like censorship on the Net, how people should behave on-line, and the possibilities for trouble if the long-distance telephone companies take over the Internet. Then the sci.classics newsgroup offers up some thoughts about Plato and his Academy, along with a silly top-this-if-you-can thread by two people whose postings I've learned not to read. Usefully, Agent makes it easy to ignore the deadweight by filtering out messages from any posters I specify. The news.answers groups is loaded, with 76 messages, all of them long documents packed with information about particular issues. These are called FAQs, for Frequently Asked Questions; they're the mission statements and backgrounders from the various newsgroups, each posted as people in the group have the time to assemble them. Good grief, what's this they're saying about Spock in alt.tv.star-trek.tos? And how do I interpret these warnings about another devaluation in Venezuela in soc.culture.venezuela (my Spanish is enthusiastic but fragmentary)? My stock there could be in trouble. Well, this could go on all morning, and the clock says I have work to do. I close Agent and double-click Netscape back into full-screen dimensions to rejoin the Web.

Putting the Web to Work

The World Wide Web has opened dramatically to commerce, as companies convert catalogs, mailing lists, press releases, television ads, and product brochures into digital format for easy access by the on-line community. My friend Cliff Allen has been there from the start. The owner of a firm that specializes in marketing for high-tech companies, Cliff designs Web pages as part of the product strategy for many of his clients. I'm checking his Web site now for updates on a project he and I have been involved with for the last two months: a competition of Web site developers. It is part of a technology fair Coopers & Lybrand will hold in Durham to discuss the whole question of technological change in the modern corporation. National in scope, the competition allows participants in the conference to submit their Web sites, which will be evaluated according to criteria that Cliff developed. As of now, we have forty-plus entries, with three stragglers still out. We're looking at several days of painstaking work going through this list link by link to arrive at our winners. I think about the fact that when a conservative accounting firm like Coopers & Lybrand embraces the Web, its use has spread so widely that no business can afford to ignore the potential on-line competition.

But back to the subject at hand: how to evaluate a Web site. The use of graphics is obviously a major feature, given the ease with which Web sites can employ them and the dangers in misusing the format; too many sites, for example, contain huge images, whose downloading when you access their home page leaves you impatiently waiting before you can proceed with your research. Cliff and I also put heavy emphasis upon interactive features, for a good site should draw the user in through possibilities like on-line forms for further information, e-mail to the company, interactive chat or discussion areas, and well-designed links between topics. We included a category for advanced technologies—some companies are experimenting with software like Sun Microsystems's Java programming language and Macromedia's Shockwave application, which provide changeable content after the Web page has been accessed, often with spectacular visual effects. Finally, we look at educational value, entertainment, and ability to motivate a potential customer.

When Cliff sends me the list of competitors, all their addresses become hyperlinks, so I can read the message and click on one or more sites to go directly to that Web page. I've clicked, for example, on a site developed by a Chapel Hill–based @dver@ctive, a company that specializes in creating interactive Web advertising (http://207.69.132.225/). @dver@ctive uses Macromedia's Shockwave add-on to Netscape to make its work livelier; on its home page, I find logos that ripple and change color, text that seems to melt and morph into a range of shapes. If the medium is indeed the message, @dver@ctive's classy Web site is a potent advertisement for the work it performs; we've already decided to give it best of show in the advanced category.

Another click takes me to the Legg Mason Investment Center (http://www.leggmason.com/), whose site will take our best of show as a sales motivator. The Baltimore firm engages in corporate and public finance, with brokerage and investment services that are amply reflected in its site. Here I can search the company's mutual fund offerings in stocks, bonds, and money market accounts, receiving updated information on performance and backgrounders on the management teams of each fund; an interactive form makes it possible to request a prospectus as well. The entire site is searchable through a keyword-driven search engine, making it simple to find the funds I need, while a clickable image map pulls up data about Legg Mason branch offices throughout the eastern seaboard.

We still have to make the call on best overall site, as well as the best interactive features winner, although clear contenders are arising in both categories. I keep clicking, reviewing sites. A travel agency, PC Travel, operating completely on-line, offers a database of air schedules and fares worldwide (http://www.pctravel.com/). A television station, WRAL here in Raleigh, updates text-based news with audio and video clips, and provides a complete range of local weather maps (http://www.wral-tv.com/). A superb entry from Lowe's, the warehouse-style home improvement retailer, contains a database of articles about everything from fixing a balky lawnmower to installing a deck on your house (http://www.lowes.com/). The choices are difficult as we come down the stretch looking for winners. I decide to think about them overnight.

During the first wave of Web development, the only businesses making money in cyberspace were the companies that sold Internet services. But that was to be expected; naturally, the Web developers themselves would be the first to turn a profit, whereas the benefits of on-line access to catalogs and databases for consumers and wholesalers wouldn't begin to appear until the Net audience reached critical mass. The sites I'm examining now indicate to me that this is happening. Their range, their sophistication, and their clear commitment to the enterprise make the case that on-line commerce is leaving its experimental stage and heading for profitability.

On-Line with the Newspaper

Morning is when I catch up on the news, and the World Wide Web is the place. I'm behind schedule with the computer column I write and need to update myself on technology stories that broke within the past 48 hours. To do this, I've slipped into *Inter@ctive Week*'s site on the World Wide Web (http://www.zdnet.com/intweek/). *IW* is a great journal if you need to track this industry, and its on-line version has the advantage of being readily clickable. I point to what I want to read and go, slipping into the news of the day before it reaches me in the print edition.

Hypertext lets me finagle news sources in ways I couldn't with any other medium. I decide to catch up on news about Java, figuring it may be of use in our Web site evaluations. *The Inter@ctive Week* Web site provides a hyperlink that points straight at Sun Micro-systems's own Web page (http://www.sun.com/). Now I'm trolling through Sun's databanks, checking out Java developments. Sun is promising that Java will become the programming language that changes how software is delivered; it may, I read, someday become the language of the Internet, a kind of universal oper-ating system. Well, of course Sun likes its product.

But I'm sliding along in an elastic news medium now; I can click over to InfoSeek (http://ultra.infoseek.com/) and run a search on the most recent Java news in its database of computer magazine titles, which turns up a solid backgrounder in another magazine, *Internet World*, which in turn offers a Web site with all its back issues archived (http://www.iworld.com/), some of which lead to Microsoft's take on Java (http://www.microsoft.com/), which isn't what you might expect, as can be verified from this hyperlinked article in *The Financial Times* . . .

I've gone pretty far afield in the space of 10 minutes, but I've managed to use the medium to my advantage. This priceless ability to call up supporting evidence or contrary opinion for any story is something that a good newspaper needs to leverage for its readers. I jump to my local paper, *The News & Observer*, which has made a name for itself by doing precisely this (http://www.nando.net/). Its technology page is laden with links to background materials like press releases and wire-service stories that support the original account in this morning's paper. The *N&O* likes sound, too; soon I'm clicking through audio files that let me hear what prominent people are saying about the latest telecommunications legislation. Not bad for a medium that, in its print form, is essentially static.

With Netscape's help, I scan the headlines, looking for anything that might tie into my writing or my investments. China and Taiwan are getting along better today, which means my stocks in Hong Kong look a bit less risky. I jump to the Hong Kong Stock Reports page and verify this, reading a quick summary of yesterday's market action on the Hang Seng. Then I link to the Center for Latin American Capital Markets Research; the center offers a link to El Universal, a Spanish-language briefing on financial news in Venezuela, where I ease my fears that devaluation is imminent.

Switching gears—easy to do with this technology—I decide to check some NCAA scores. And I know just the place: The WRAL site we are evaluating for the Web competition can provide me with video from the Wake Forest game. WRAL also shows me a weather map based on a satellite image taken about an hour ago. That cold front now crossing the mountains looks like it will bring rain. And, as if to prove the point, the trees outside have begun to sway in a sudden breeze, the pines furling nicely at their points, the wind chimes ringing.

I've got the news I need for the moment; I can get a computer column out of the Java Cup competition whose winners were announced today. I've downloaded the story and it's printing out as I write this.

Down the Rabbit Hole and into the Mailbox

My physical mailbox, the one that keeps getting knocked over when people turn around in the driveway across the street and back into it, is getting to be less of a factor than ever. Most of my physical mail—come-ons from credit card companies, computer magazines, catalogs, brochures—gets thrown out, a tremendous waste of paper and print resources. On-line, you don't run into this kind of thing. If junk mail comes, and I get growing amounts of it on-line, it's easy to discard. I hit a key combination—Ctrl-D, for my software—and the offending message is blasted into digitalia. Most of the messages I do receive are usually on target. They're from people I know, correspondents who keep in touch through electronic mail far more frequently than they would call on the phone or write physical letters. That's one of the phenomena of cyberspace, the fact that people seem energized by it.

With Netscape minimized in the corner of my screen, I launch the Eudora mail reader. Eudora is a personal favorite, a freeware product with a commercial upgrade from a company called QUALCOMM Incorporated. On-screen, it's an unremarkable thing; no visual effects to speak of, no animation or moving video. But it's an enabler. It lets me pull down a menu to retrieve my mail and then sort the day's worth by subject.

At my command, Eudora taps into my service provider's mail server. The mail server is a computer dedicated to the process of mail delivery; it stores mail that arrives while I'm not on-line and holds it for me as long as necessary. The next time I log on, the server sends me the waiting queue, which Eudora then assists me in answering. The process is managed by so-called Post Office Protocol, or POP. The analogy is reasonably exact; the server acts like the post office, sans federal employees; it's the place where the mail arrives and waits for local delivery. I can initiate that delivery whenever I choose.

Only my computer and the network see this protocol; I see the client programs like Netscape and Eudora. Most modern clients use the windows (small *w*) format, whether you use a Mac or an Intel-based PC; they provide drop-down menus, mouse-click commands, and help systems that point you in the right way when you're lost. True, you've got to configure them; the newsreader I used earlier had to be told the address of the news server it was using, just as Eudora needs to know which server to hit to get the mail. But that information is given to you by your service provider. All you need to do is to pull down the configuration menu in each case and insert the address.

And now it's mail time. When I type in my mailbox password, Eudora starts negotiating with the server, which starts sending mail. Soon a chime sounds, and I'm presented with a list of messages. Here's one from a friend who's planning to have lunch with me next week; he's a state government employee with a penchant for linguistics. Here's a reminder that another friend is planning a party to watch the Oscar awards ceremony; I should dress like a movie star for the occasion. Here's a message from a mailing list about computers in society, bemoaning the callous way certain journalists have found to excuse the depredations of the Unabomber. And another mailing list message, this one explaining how to avoid oxidation in opened bottles of wine (I do a radio show on wine). Then a message from an Australian, advising me of the existence of a new list of service providers in his country.

As I go through these messages, it's with an eye toward proper disposal. Most don't need to be saved, but those that do I will want to be able to find later. For them, Eudora enables me to set up folders and subfolders; transferring messages from one to another is a matter of menu-clicking. I begin to move messages around; out go three, while two others go into my Readers folder, subcategorized by book; the one about the Oscars I leave purposefully in my "Inbox" so that I'll be reminded next time I check the mail to get out my tux. The mailing list messages are varied in their interest, but only one of them, about the impact of the Internet upon education, deserves saving for possible use in a future computer column. I've established a separate folder for column materials.

Several of these messages deserve replies, but first I intend to send some fresh mail. An editor would like to know that a story I'm writing about networking and education is on schedule. Thankfully, I don't have to remember everybody's e-mail address. Eudora lets me set up nicknames. All I have to do is type my editor's first name—Regina—and Eudora supplies the rest. I'm popped into an outgoing message box with the cursor ready to supply a subject in the appropriate field. I've learned to stick with first names when establishing nicknames, instead of getting too fanciful—otherwise, I forget who is who.

I also send a message to subscribe to a mailing list about the history of cyberspace. The mailing list is maintained at a computer run by the organization called Computer Professionals for Social Responsibility. Computers that run mailing lists are frequently called listservs, after the program they use to handle these chores. I subscribe to the group by sending mail to this address: listserv@cpsr.org (note that the term *listserv* appears in the address itself). Because this particular mailing list handles subscriptions by machine instead of a person, I send a formulaic message: subscribe cpsr-history paul gilster. The listserv will add me to the subscription list and I'll start receiving mail.

Mailing lists are one of the most underutilized resources on the Internet. Like the newsgroups, they exist for thousands of topics; whatever your interest, there's probably a list about it. When you sign up, you start receiving the various messages these people send to each other in your mailbox, and you can reply as well. Some lists are relatively lighthearted, while some are scholarly discussions so deep that only experts can follow them. What I like about these lists, aside from their obvious uses in learning more about

a subject and being able to consult with knowledge-
able people, is the sense of community they inspire.
Put all the Border Collie owners on a mailing list, for
instance, and you create not only a valuable pool of
information but a geographically dispersed group of
acquaintances and, eventually, friends. They'll solve a
problem or provide a sympathetic ear when your own
dog is acting flaky, which among Border Collies is
most of the time.

Going to the Chapel

High technology and daily life mix intriguingly on
today's Internet, a welcome outcome of the Net's great
democratization. My daughter's wedding is a case in
point. Being global, the Internet doesn't suggest itself
as a resource for such an emphatically local event. On
the other hand, running searches through a constantly expanding cyberspace routinely generates
surprises, so I pause to log on to Yahoo!, the directory
and search site that is perhaps the most visible of all
the proliferating search engines (http://www.yahoo.
com/). The work of two Stanford students who have
managed to make it into a publicly traded company,
Yahoo! usefully breaks down Net sites by topic. It's
a sure route for beginners to explore, and an entry
point for seasoned researchers trying to get a quick
overview on their topic.

Yahoo! lets me search by keyword as well, so I opt
to combine strategies. Entering "weddings" as my keyword, I click the search button to run the keyword
against the Yahoo! database. Numerous hits appear,
almost 200 of them, but that's not surprising; the key-

word is doubtless turning up at many of these sites as a mere mention in a paragraph rather than as the object of the page's existence. But at the top of the list of hits, an advertisement appears that seems to be directed right at me. It reads "Is your wedding a) in a limo, or b) in limbo? bridalnet.com." Thus the power of the search engine for marketers; its developers can sell certain keywords, like "weddings," to advertisers, who now know that their ad will appear before the eyes of anyone searching under that keyword. Internet advertising targets potential customers like a cruise missile.

The ad is clickable, so I soon find myself at the Bridal Net home page, a wondrous creation in pink and pastels, that offers bridal registry services; fill out the form and your wishes are recorded for the benefit of out-of-town guests with Internet accounts. Listings of travel agents and honeymoon destinations provide links to their respective businesses. A clickable image map of the United States yields wedding services available in North Carolina, some local, some national distributors. Using the map, I locate a discount wedding invitation dealer, a florist, a purveyor of groomsmen's gifts, a candlemaker, a table linen rental service that ships nationwide, and a wedding photographer.

A little more digital travel takes me further afield. The Civil Rites & Ceremonies page is the work of Hilary Hudson, a justice of the peace in New Zealand who has written a book of the same name. Hudson's book includes readings from 50 variant ceremonies celebrating weddings in and out of the established churches. The GRAPEvine Catering Company home page turns out to be right here in Raleigh. Soon I'm examining hot entrée possibilities for the reception. Artichoke-filled chicken rolls vie with sliced sirloin with shallot wine sauce or a pasta primavera for the vegetarians. The GRAPEvine also handles deep-dish spanokopita, one of my favorite Greek items, and side dishes ranging from oven-roasted garlic potatoes to seasoned sesame noodles.

I bookmark the site for my wife to examine; fathers of the bride can't be too forward in making their recommendations. Here's The Guide Book to Wedding Photography for the Advanced Amateur. It's the production of Allan Ross Photography; I can find out about aperture and shutter speeds in a darkened church, how to control background and foreground light, how to allocate film and set up equipment, and if Ross is to be believed, I can save several hundred dollars in the process. A click will order this book, but I lack confidence in my shutter skills. A switch to the InfoSeek search engine pulls up a professional, G&R Photography in Chapel Hill, just down the road. Samples of their work are offered on their Web page, and they seem to specialize in weddings.

Search engines are like this: Each searches its own database, so that a thorough investigation into any topic usually involves multiple sites. InfoSeek likewise pulls up the Triangle Wedding Services page, also right here in Raleigh. It provides something we've been needing, a schedule that breaks down what we should be doing every step of the way as we plan for the big day. The wedding being three months away, the guide recommends that we should already have finalized our guest list and taken the wedding portrait (we're slow on that one). Planning lodging for out-of-town guests is also sneaking up on us, according to Triangle Wedding Services. But the Raleigh-based Wedding and Party Pros Disk Jockey page promises to handle all our music needs. And here's a trumpeter, one Timothy Dore, who has experience with the University of North Carolina Brass Ensemble. He offers a classical music touch—and he included selected clips of his work. After listening to his moves on Charpentier's *Te Deum*, my wife and I decide to send him e-mail, hoping he may be available for the event.

Putting the Multi in Media

Dore's music clips remind me to check into the RealAudio home page (http://www.realaudio.com/). RealAudio is the brainchild of a company called Progressive Networks, which has dreamed up a way to send radio and other audio programming over the Internet. What I like about RealAudio is that it lets me log on and start listening immediately, without downloading a lengthy sound file and playing it back later. I check the selections on RealAudio's home page and decide it's time to see what National Public Radio has aired in the last few days.

The beauty of combining radio with computers is that the programming becomes fully switchable. You can look through a catalog of shows and choose the one you want. It's as easy to archive radio shows in this format as it is to create a database of text files. The benefits are legion. Too much good programming crosses the air for me to listen to more than a fraction of it—who has the time? At the National Public Radio archive, I can browse the index of shows like *All Things Considered*, *Science Friday*, and *Talk of the Nation*. This is particularly useful for me, since telecommunications issues and the growth of the cyberculture periodically interest the NPR producers.

I can call up an hour-long discussion about ENIAC, the world's first general-purpose computer, whose 18,000 vacuum tubes defined the state of the art in the late 1940s. Authors Joel Shurkin and Sherry Turkle join the University of Pennsylvania's Mitchell Marcus for the conversation. Or I can request a roundtable about regulatory reform as we move into a world where telephone companies begin to compete with cable television carriers; MIT's Andrew Lippman and the FCC's Richard Wiley are key players in this debate.

Not everything is quite so serious. Here's an *All Things Considered* story on Spring Street Brewing, a New York–based microbrewery that has set up a unique stock trading system on the Internet. A click on its hyperlink pops up the RealAudio program, which appears as a small box with controls like those on a CD player. Quickly I'm listening to NPR's Jim Zarroli talking about the Securities and Exchange Commission's reaction to Spring Street's initiative, the sound surprisingly clear considering that it has been digitized, packetized, and fed through myriad routers on its way to my desk.

Switchable audio, however, can play havoc with your work schedule. In my case, I could get into trouble listening to the show on the physics of *Star Trek*; better avoid the temptation to get into that one or I won't get anything done for the rest of the hour. But when the Spring Street show ends, I could use some music, so I zip over to the AudioNet home page (http://www.audionet.com/), where everything from audio books to live radio is displayed on a comprehensive menu. There's an Eagles' Greatest Hits CD in the AudioNet jukebox, so within minutes I'm back in Microsoft Word working on this book while "Hotel

California" plays through the speakers. Later, I'll update the news with a check on the live radio feed from CKUA in Edmonton, Alberta.

What I really need is a microphone, I'm thinking as I look outside at a stunning Carolina afternoon, white cumulus puffs scudding through a painted sky. A microphone would let me use Internet Phone, a product from Vocaltec that likewise digitizes audio for packetizing and transmission over the Net. But with Internet Phone, I can connect to any other user who has the software and a microphone to surmount the limitations of the long-distance telephone system (namely, price) by talking at no charge other than the monthly Internet access fee I pay anyway. Internet Phone is remarkable stuff; I've seen it demonstrated at one of the Internet World shows, and it points to a future where the transmission mechanism is less important than the content it carries. No wonder the telephone companies are keeping such a close eye on this stuff, and no wonder they're forming alliances with content companies like Disney and Paramount. Suddenly moviemakers are digital players, and content, not transmission, is where the action is.

Thinking about Vocaltec and Internet Phone has me wondering whether I couldn't slip out tonight to the local Radio Shack to pick up a microphone. If so, I'll need the Internet Phone software, but that's not a problem. More and more companies are either giving their software away to gain market share, or are offering "light" versions of their programs, fully functional applications that you can upgrade if you think you need more capabilities. Eudora, the mail program, is like that; I've used the free version in the past but have upgraded because the commercial Eudora offers an enhanced set of features.

Surely Vocaltec offers Internet Phone in some accessible fashion. But where is Vocaltec? This is the kind of question that used to baffle Internet users; here we were with a globe-spanning network of computers, thousands of which offered data, programs, and graphics of all kinds, only we had no way of knowing what was where. Today, I can just call up one of the Internet search engines and quickly track down the source. When I enter my keywords, "internet phone," into the InfoSeek database, using quotation marks to tell the search engine that I want to see a list of all Web documents in which these words appear next to each other, I am answered with a list of hyperlinks pointing to the Vocaltec site (http://www.vocaltec.com/).

A click and I'm there. Sure enough, the first thing that greets me on this page is a banner that proclaims, among other things, "Download a Free Copy!" The link provides the gateway into the Vocaltec file download site. Netscape pops up a window asking where I want to put this acquisition, offering me a choice of possible destinations on my hard disk. I take the default and soon am watching the download proceed. When it's complete, I'll have Internet phone on my machine in compressed form. Most Internet software comes this way; usually, you simply run the program, which decompresses itself and provides you with a setup program. Run that and the software is installed.

The download is quick; despite its capabilities, Internet Phone isn't a huge file. A double-click on its icon in Windows Explorer runs the executable program, which unpacks the various files. A double-click on the Setup icon runs the installation. Setup asks me which directory I want to put the program in and then lets me create an appropriate one, after which it installs the program and creates an icon for it. I make sure to leave a copy of the original executable file I downloaded in the Internet Phone directory. That way, I will have a clean copy ready to be reinstalled in case of trouble.

With the setup complete, I suddenly remember that NBC Desktop Video has scheduled a speech by Alan Greenspan on the economy this afternoon. I want to hear Greenspan because my typical Internet day involves keeping an eye on the stock market. But I have a few minutes, so I jump to the Xing Technology page in Arroyo, California (http://www.xingtech. com/). Xing has lined up content from all over the globe in a multitude of formats: Bavarian radio, live television from Finland, NetSource Radio from France. I'm enjoying the browse, but it's approaching 3:00; if I'm going to watch Greenspan, I need to activate the company's StreamWorks client, which I downloaded and installed several weeks ago.

As you might imagine, when video is sent through the packet-switched Internet, we're accomplishing quite a feat. Video is a demanding type of content; live transmission requires all kinds of tricks to compress the information so that it can flow within the constraints of our Internet connections. Xing's take on all this is to offer different rates of video, each ideal for a particular type of connection. The NBC Desktop Video link offers me a choice of speeds, from which I choose 24Kbps because it's marked as the one for 28.8 modem users to try. A modem gives you a slower frame rate than a high-speed connection; the frames slide jerkily into each other. It's hardly cable television, but it is a demonstration that as we continue to expand the Internet's data pipes, all kinds of content will become available. After all, a data packet doesn't care what it's carrying.

Up on the screen pops an image of Lucio Noto, the chairman and CEO of Mobil Corporation, discussing Mobil's operations abroad, with radio-quality audio. I'm given a series of clickable buttons for Xing options, including setup screens and links to popular sites. NBC Desktop Video is one of the early players in the futuristic world of cyberspace television. The service pumps live reports on breaking news and events that can move the markets onto the Internet, including corporate press conferences and Federal Reserve statements. For those of us who play the market, such events can provide clues that could change the weighting in our portfolios, or at least give us enough background information to form some insights into the economy. I don't need to know Lucio Noto's views on shareholder value because I don't hold Mobil stock, but Alan Greenspan's thoughts on interest rates ought to be interesting. Interest rates, after all, move markets.

Into the Realm of Virtual Reality

It's 3:30 now; I've managed to keep writing while Greenspan spoke in the background, a sort of mental multitasking that Internet users quickly master. Interest rates look unchangeable for the moment, so I'm not planning any sudden moves with my stocks. Besides, I have an appointment to check into a virtual world to meet a cyberperson. Virtual reality is the latest thing in computer interfaces; it's the creation of on-line environments that mimic the shapes and colors of the physical world. Some virtual reality environments exist to provide gateways to information in database or other form, but at the present, most are experimental, pushing the limits of the medium to explore the possibilities. They allow you to work with the entire palate of Internet tools—animation, sound, video, music, and, of course, text—all within a vividly realized screen world through which you navigate with mouse movements. Push the mouse forward to ease deeper into the scene, slide it right or left to turn. The screen redraws, crudely but enticingly, as you move.

Some people think virtual reality will be the model for all future browsers. The idea is that it's easier to manipulate a world that offers genuine analogues with our own than to adapt to even the most intuitive user interface. Which would you find easier to use, a system with a desktop metaphor that requires you to pull down menus and make selections to accomplish your work, or a virtual world that looks like your office, and in which you maneuver by using your mouse and keyboard? How about a virtual world in which the scenery is an artist's conception of an alien planet, with fantastic buildings representing various data repositories and gateways to interactive chat rooms? Instead of finding and clicking on a destination, you would move your mouse. Your view would alter so that you seemed to be actually approaching and then entering the building. Inside, you could find your information by browsing among virtual bookshelves, or run a search by asking a virtual librarian for help, inserting the appropriate keywords as needed. Maybe you would visit a museum and be able to walk freely along its corridors, stopping to view whichever painting you chose. How about a trip through the inside of a nuclear reactor, or a flight aboard a digital prototype of a new airliner?

You can also imagine a virtual world where you not only move about and interact with objects, but create content as well. Imagine building your own structures within this environment, setting up shop in a virtual building in which you could display your business catalog or readings from your favorite poet. The world you moved through might not look precisely like our world, but its multidimensional capabilities would transcend the flat and linear computer screen to take you into a world of up, down, sideways, and through.

In Neal Stephenson's book *Snow Crash*, the characters frequent a cyberworld called the Metaverse, in which each has an "avatar," a digital representation of the person behind the connection. Having moved into the virtual space, the individual is surrounded by a three-dimensional representation of a digital boulevard, the Street, complete with buildings, sidewalks, and pedestrians. Each "person" in the display is someone's avatar, a fellow cybercitizen likewise on-line. Real business takes place in the digital boulevard; relationships are formed, plots hatched, ideas exchanged. The virtual world becomes an alternate reality, a parallel universe that's as close as the nearest network jack.

Hiro, Stephenson's protagonist, jacks into the Metaverse frequently; much of the action in *Snow Crash* takes place in this striking setting: "It is a hundred meters wide, with a narrow monorail track running down the middle. The monorail is a free piece of public utility software that enables users to change their location on the Street rapidly and smoothly. A lot of people just ride back and forth on it, looking at the sights. When Hiro first saw this place, ten years ago, the monorail hadn't been written yet; he and his buddies had to write car and motorcycle software in order to get around. They would take their software out and race it in the black desert of the electronic night."[1]

Stephenson's vision of the 3-D cyberworld isn't here yet, but right now I'm logging on to something called Worlds Chat (http://www.worlds.net/), where I have an appointment with a source for my article about the future of computers in education. He's David Warlick, a computer consultant who is convinced that virtual worlds hold great promise for schoolchildren. Put them into such a world with the appropriate tools and they can experiment on reality with remarkable verisimilitude and little risk. David's opinions are valuable to me because his background in education is extensive; he has already helped to set up text-based virtual worlds in which children have been able to build structures and interact on-line. He has even built a digital school within the bowels of a Sun workstation downtown, all via an earlier generation of text-based software.

We're to meet at 4:00, so I have to move fast. I launch the Worlds Chat software and enter the Avatar Gallery. The Worlds Chat software offers a variety of appearances; I can be anything from a scholarly looking man in a business suit to a gold and vermilion butterfly. Shopping for avatars is an eerie experience; you find yourself in a showroom in which the various avatar bodies are displayed like museum paintings; they can be rotated and examined to make sure you've got the one you really want. Pick your avatar and you're ready to go on-line, launching yourself into a futuristic space station with multiple hubs and spokes. Which I now do, finding myself standing in a large room populated with avatars moving in a seemingly dreamlike trance. A girl who looks like Alice in Wonderland is here, as is a penguin, and a woman with flaming red hair and a black dress. A chess piece glides past.

David and I have agreed to "meet" over by the Alpha World sign, which I can see in the corner. I "walk" there by moving my mouse in slow up-and-down motions that take me across the floor, dodging my fellow avatars as I go. In an amusing conflation of virtual reality and the deeper realities of today's network, each of these avatars bears a name above its head, a textual reminder of identity. The penguin is named Woody; the red-haired woman is Black Rose. When I "speak" to Black Rose, I do so by typing into a text box that appears below the virtual scene. She "answers" in the same fashion, and now we're typing back and forth, just like two people connected by a keyboard in a standard chat room. We haven't yet reached the point where full audio and video capabilities can be injected into a virtual scene, although it can't be long before that future arrives.

David's avatar is not quite like him, but it's close, a young man with jeans and a flannel shirt who waits for me in the corner. "Nice to see you," he types as I approach, and we stand face to face, our avatars motionless as we talk. I don't find this kind of interviewing easy to conduct. The limitation of typing at someone is that you can never keep up the pace; your thoughts always outrun your fingers. On the other hand, the venue seems precisely right for discussing the modeling of virtual environments. Our conversation dispenses with pleasantries; we zero in on the purpose of this meeting, which is to figure out what impact digital networking will have on the way our children learn.

Of course, we're shooting in the dark. I suspect we can't even begin to imagine how this technology, translated years ahead, will affect basic social interactions like education. Clearly, we have to dream up new

instructional models in this environment, because
the lecturer/student model—the broadcast model of
teaching, if you will—is being replaced by a format
that stresses acquiring search abilities and learning
the critical skills necessary to evaluate differing types
of content. Perhaps the teacher becomes more of a
mediator, a facilitator, and less of a dispenser of
knowledge, but if that is the case, what does it say
about the apprentice model that has served human
culture throughout history? Yes, education must
change, but what must change the most is ourselves.

Catching up with the Galaxy

But I have an educational agenda of my own this
afternoon, and having agreed to renew my on-line
conversation with David later in the week, I leave
Worlds Chat to reenter the Web, where I find myself in
Professor Greg Bothun's class Astronomy 123, called
Cosmology and the Origin of Life. Bothun teaches at
the University of Oregon, and makes his course available on the Internet. Of course, I'm not enrolled at the
university; instead, I'm considering becoming an
auditor, looking over the professor's shoulder electronically. I'm here today to see how the class is struc-
tured.

Astronomy 123 is an attempt to push the limits of
the networking medium. All lectures in the course are
to be delivered electronically, supplemented by the
optional textbook *The Search for Life in the Universe*,
by Goldsmith and Owen. The lecture pages themselves
are in Netscape format (by this, Bothun means he has
prepared them using Netscape's HTML extensions

that allow particular features, like forms, to be present on Web pages displayed by the browser). Bothun is methodical; his Web pages lay out the course with precision. Clicking through the schedule, I find that the first section discusses historical cosmologies, the way early cultures looked at the universe. The standard model of the universe accepted by physicists today comes next, while section three considers how the earth formed and studies the evolution of life. The provocative fourth part examines life beyond our planet and the possibilities for contacting it.

Bothun lists a number of reasons for using the Internet as the medium for his class. Because astronomical information is plentiful on the Net, an on-line course allows easy movement between the class and outside information caches. More controversially, Bothun argues that placing course materials on-line means that students won't have to take notes; after all, why try to duplicate what the professor has already made available in full form to all students? I pause on this one, thinking that the value of note-taking is that it forces you to translate ideas. When I take notes, I'm compelled to understand what it is I'm studying. Writing amplifies the necessary process of comprehension. If students don't engage in this process, will they learn as effectively?

Experiments like this one will help to answer that question. But on a final benefit of Net-based teaching, I agree with Bothun, who argues that the computer environment will foster a better flow of ideas between students and professor. In classes I've taught, I've always found three kinds of students: those that participate actively; those who can be coaxed into occasional comment; and those who don't participate at all. The last group, the ones who sit at the back of the class, is composed of all kinds of students, from those who simply shouldn't be there to those who are brilliant but too shy or inwardly focused to talk freely. Reaching these students can be a teacher's most rewarding experience, opening them up to creativity and learning.

Computers can help us do this. I've seen the principle tested with workgroup software at one of IBM's sites in Raleigh, noting that when people are given the chance to express themselves digitally, without facial expressions or eye contact, they tend to speak more freely.[2] A group engaged in this kind of discussion can count on a wider representation from its quieter members, while questions that might not be asked out of embarrassment in front of a class can be added to the agenda through private e-mail between professors and students. They can then be debated by the entire class through on-line newsgroups and discussion areas, both of which Bothun makes available.

As an electronic auditor, I would be limited in being able to work through the lecture notes alone. Yet the possibilities are still powerful. Bothun has set up links to cosmology sites elsewhere on the Net, from the National Center for Supercomputing Applications' Cosmos in a Computer exhibit to a cosmology page at Iowa State University that contains tutorials on astronomical subjects, including a three-part teaching sequence on the Big Bang. One link leads to the home page for the Hubble Space Telescope, another to an interactive table of the elements, a third to a primer on galactic structure.

If I'm diligent, I can use these pages as supplements to the on-line lectures, which are laid out in a logical sequence beginning with early creation myths. Clicking my way into these pages, I'm now into a set of notes interspersed with diagrams, looking at everything from the Greek view of the gods to thermonuclear fusion in various types of stars; the latter subject is neatly supplemented by a series of photographs from various Internet sites showing examples of such phenomena as Supernova 1994I and SN 1993J. As the lecture notes point out, the abundance of iron from these explosions played a material role in developing the properties of the heavy planets, making them suitable for the evolution of life. Diagrams explain helium fusion in stars, with visual and audio support. The formation of Earth's atmosphere and the appearance of the first life-forms is told through an interlinking set of illustrated notes.

What's interesting about sites like this is that they make available material that would otherwise have been closed, sidestepping the traditional educational hierarchy. Add to this the beauty of archived classes. When you teach a class on-line and compile not only lecture notes but links to multimedia resources and other data, the entire compilation can remain available on the Internet. Such collections can become a data bank that people can use as lifelong learning tools. Free of campus politics, the best teachers and the most valuable sites should rise to the top, a phenomenon not always found in a world where tenure too easily becomes a shield to protect the incompetent.

Yes, this course seems to be worth following, I muse as I check my electronic mail for the last time today. There being no time constraint, I can sit in on Astronomy 123 as necessary to pursue the lecture notes, which gives me the freedom to sandwich my study of cosmological theory around an increasingly hectic work schedule. Education on the Internet is a grand experiment; we can only try different approaches to see which are the most vital. True, closing the gap between society and its educational institutions isn't something the Internet was designed to do, but as in so many other areas, electronic networking demonstrates a flexible and largely untapped potential.

Twilight on the Internet

I've got one more thing to do before shutting down this evening: a quick hop over to Amazon.com, an on-line bookstore that makes ordering books a snap. The company, based in Seattle, provides a database of 1 million titles, with on-line ordering and free notification service; it's a combined search engine and store for bookish people (http://www.amazon.com/). I'm hunting for a book by Masanobu Tsuji, the architect of Japan's brilliant triumph over the British at Singapore in 1941. Tsuji was the general who understood the fortress mentality prevailing on the island; his plan brought General Yamashita's troops down the Malay peninsula through supposedly impassable jungle, positioning them on the back side of the big seaward-facing guns. You would think a successful career as an author would have kept him in the public eye, but he was publicly seen for the last time somewhere in Thailand in the mid 1970s, an enigmatic and fascinating figure.

Tsuji's account of the Singapore campaign, available in Japan, has only recently made it into print in the United States, and it has been hard to find; the only copy I've located was so dog-eared that I decided against it. I log on to the Amazon.com site to search under the author category, running the name Tsuji past the search engine here. Quickly, 15 titles pop up, including the one I'm seeking: *Japan's Greatest Victory, Britain's Worst Defeat*, an English translation of Tsuji's work by Margaret Lake. A click deposits the book in my on-line shopping basket. Then it's a quick run back to the search engine for David Moskowitz's *OS/2 Unleashed*, which I need to help me configure and fine-tune the OS/2 operating system on my ThinkPad. I add it to my shopping basket as well. A final search lets me check whether the latest volume of Norman Sherry's biography of Graham Greene has yet become available in the United States. No trace of it yet.

As you can see, Amazon.com is something of a browser's paradise. I am one of those people who cannot walk past a bookstore, particularly if it houses used books; I love things that are hard to find and bear the mark of long acquaintance. Amazon.com doesn't sell used books, but its million-title catalog is large enough that I can track down arcane titles like Tsuji's. The temptation is to linger on this page and keep feeding the search engine authors and titles, before the realization sinks home that in a bookstore of this depth, I could burn up several hundred dollars buying books in a few minutes. It's time to close up shop for the day.

Logging out of the Internet involves clicking my software's Disconnect button, which in turn breaks the telephone connection and shuts down the TCP/IP protocols that allowed the Net to flow through my computer. Modem users don't leave their machines on the Net full-time even when they're paying flat rate. If I had a dedicated Internet connection—a full-time hookup over a special circuit—I could set up my machine as a server, posting material on a Web site or maintaining a mailing list. You would think you could do that with a PPP connection and a flat-rate account; after all, aren't you paying the same amount whether you're on for 20 minutes or 20 hours?

The answer is, your payments are the same, but the dynamic addressing scheme most flat-rate providers put in place means that your IP address changes every time you log on. You never know what it will be because it's assigned by computer. And that means that even if you set up as a server, no one would know where to find you because you'd be a moving target. You can see why the providers have to manage things this way. If you want a full-time network address, you need to pay for it, in their view, and since they've got the tools that make it work, who are we to argue? So most of us use our modems to help us become on-line researchers, consumers of information, confining our publishing to venues like electronic mail, mailing lists, and newsgroups. The next step up, a personal Web page on our provider's computer, would cost more (although even this is changing as commercial information services like CompuServe experiment with limited Web publishing for their customers).

But I'm still thinking about books. Masanobu Tsuji, Graham Greene, and OS/2. The on-line search engine has let me race through a million titles to find just the ones I need. There is something in this that confirms my enthusiasm about the Internet in general. Specifically, it's a place where diversity rules. I'm shutting down my system now, but I'm thinking that the freedom to move between ideas is the Net's great attraction. What it offers in this regard does not replace conventional reading or scholarship, but takes both into new territory. Publishers won't regret putting material on-line because they aren't going to lose old readers so much as gain new ones. The act of on-line reading is fundamentally different than the act of reading a bound book.

My five-volume set of Dryden's Plutarch translation is a treasure; I open it by the fire and enjoy it on chilly fall evenings while I sip a glass of wine. The texture of the book cover in my hand, the smell of 75-year-old paper and print, the sight of handsome lexicography—all these things become an immeasurably significant part of the reading experience. But I want Plutarch on-line, too. I won't read him sequentially when I'm on the Internet (who would want to, given how trying that can be on your eyes?), but I'll gladly jump into a Web site or a Gopher and search his work by keyword. Happens all the time—I remember a quote, a key passage, and want to find it fast. You just can't do that kind of thing with a bound book, which is what will promote the intertwining of content, digital and analog, that holds so much promise for the coming century.

Content Evaluation

When image becomes substance, and the picture all too often substitutes for the thousand words that would more accurately describe an event or an idea, the audience is in danger of being misled.

When is a globe-spanning information network dangerous? When people make too many assumptions about what they find on it. For while the Internet offers myriad opportunities for learning, an unconsidered view of its contents can be misleading and deceptive. This is why critical thinking about content is the Internet competency upon which all others are founded. You cannot work comfortably within this medium until you have established methods for judging the reliability of Web pages, newsgroup postings, and mailing lists, a task complicated by the nature of the international data flow.

Consider this story, discussed recently at an awards dinner for the American Association for Forensic Science. A man reportedly jumped from the tenth floor of a building, but before hitting the ground, he was killed by a shotgun blast fired out a ninth floor window. The shooter on the ninth floor was a man threatening his wife with the shotgun—which he believed to be unloaded. But in fact, the gun had been loaded six months earlier by the man's son, angry at his disinheritance by his mother, and intending to trick his father into killing his mother with it. When his plan failed, he decided to commit suicide by jumping from the tenth floor, but was thus killed by the very gun he had loaded.

Sound unbelievable? Nevertheless, this story was widely propagated on the Internet newsgroups.[1] From an initial posting on the Internet, at a time and place now lost, the tale gained a life of its own. Credibility grew as it echoed around the world by e-mail and newsgroup. Newspapers picked up on the plot; in fact, I first ran across it in my local paper, *The News & Observer*, here in Raleigh. Thousands of people accepted this myth as reality. The truth is that the past president of the American Academy of Forensic Sciences made up the story as part of a speech he gave in 1987.

I relate this story to illustrate the power of electronic networking. If even a small percentage of the people who read this account assumed it was true, they could use the Net to circulate it. One convincing poster could cause a ripple effect as other people read and accepted his or her conclusions uncritically. People are remarkably malleable; they tend to believe what they are told by whatever medium they're accessing, presumably out of their implicit trust in the editorial function of editors and news organizations. Unfortunately, because the Internet lacks such editorial functions, its decentralization makes the idea of news "organization" in the on-line sense a dubious proposition, as Pierre Salinger ought to have known.

This is not to say that there are no reputable news sites on the Internet; in fact, the number of trustworthy sources for everything from world affairs to financial analysis and political commentary is growing daily. But we must come to terms with the fact that for every *Wall Street Journal* and *New York Times* on the Net, there are thousands of individuals who have the opportunity to publish with impunity and certainly without editorial scrutiny. The Net is a straight shot for anyone to use sophisticated (and often free) software as a conduit of content. This puts the onus upon the reader to develop the critical skills necessary to evaluate such materials.

Separating Form from Content

Much of the Internet's spin on information is deceptively enticing. For while the World Wide Web has opened numerous doors for the providers of content, multimedia has also put the digitally illiterate user at a disadvantage. When image becomes substance, and the picture all too often substitutes for the thousand words that would more accurately describe an event or an idea, the audience is in danger of being misled. Dress up a bogus story with professional-looking fonts and photographs, blend in a snippet of audio or video, and you lend your tale a verisimilitude that it may not in fact possess.

Let's say you read an article in *Fortune* or *Investor's Business Daily* about a hot stock prospect. Chances are you'd give it some credence. But what if you saw the same tip reported in a cheaply printed flyer delivered through the mail or posted on a bulletin board at your grocery store? The same information is available in each, but we view the content differently based on presentation. Assumptions thus become an inseparable part of how we read. We must track this tendency as we explore the Internet, for—on the World Wide Web in particular—implied content can be deceptive. One of the challenges of Internet publishing is that it turns our conventional expectations, built upon years of experience with newspapers and magazines, on their head. We can no longer assume that the appearance of a publication is necessarily relevant to the quality of its information.

For instance, I can create a handsome Web page with a little study of the nondemanding HTML language and a variety of freeware editors that allow me to create content on the fly. I have seen Web pages that rival those of the most experienced developers implemented by one-person offices with a determination to use the Internet for commerce. Extremists defend everything from the Oklahoma City bombing to the Holocaust on finely tuned Web pages. Simply put, the Internet demands that our judgments about content be affected less by appearance than by our ability to evaluate and verify what we see. The diversity of Web content and its ability to be linked to other information sources provides us with unique challenges in this regard, but fortunately, it also furnishes us with the set of digital tools we need to solve the problem.

Ironically, the same issue is raised *in reverse* with text-based network resources. For most of its life, the Net has been a carrier of textual information; until recently, what you saw on the screen was simple ASCII code, unadorned with pictures and incapable of carrying the professional-looking formatting of Web pages. Straight text is a transparent carrier; alike for all concepts, it fades behind the idea, yielding to the force of the thing expressed. For these reasons, text seems to be both more honest and thus safer than multimedia.

But the problem of perception remains. While text flattens the reading space so that content can be evaluated for what it is, the written word is nonetheless composed of a limited number of symbols. When imposed on a screen's glowing phosphors, text loses the subtle cues that give us indications about how much work went into the job of publishing, and hence how seriously the publisher took his or her mission. These are judgments we make as a matter of course with printed materials; without them, we must acquire the critical skills that allow us to question attribution, authority, and references.

The modern Internet, design-rich, performs the same feat. Make multimedia ubiquitous and you flatten the perspective by enabling anyone to create a richly developed context for his or her work. Thus a willingness to challenge ideas must prevail, a deliberate and thoughtful effort to separate form from content to consider the clockwork of meaning within.

Any teacher who has used the Internet in a classroom setting can tell you how troubling it is to see children taking World Wide Web pages at face value, without the evaluative skills to place them in context. In that sense, the Internet can, in the wrong hands, become a tool of propaganda. You could consider the Internet as a wire service, at least on a superficial level. The amount of content it offers is remarkable, so that hunting through it in search of particular information requires the same kind of filtering on the part of the individual that news organizations provide on a professional level. But—and this is a big but—unlike a wire service, its content has not been chosen by professionals who can distance themselves from the motives of the creators of the news. The Internet is like a raw data stream, an open microphone for every interest group, corporation, fan club, professional organization, or fanatic that wants to use it. And if you've ever been near a karaoke club, you know how painful an open microphone can be.

Check It Out

When I do research at a public library, I have to know who is responsible for the material I find there. Any printed volume will contain this authorial information, which can be weighed in terms of that person's background and experience to determine how useful a source the book or journal article is. Similarly, every newspaper story will contain a byline.

The expectation of a byline is frequently unmet on the Internet. In search of materials about Ashanti Gold, a mining company whose fortunes in Ghana had attracted my interest as an investor, I was able to use a search engine to locate numerous sites, including one that gave me a complete breakdown of Ashanti's current financial condition and its prospects for the coming year. But missing from this wealth of information was the source. Did this material come from an annual report? Was it written by a shareholder, or a member of the board of directors? Could it have been planted by a competitor, with the potential for distorting the company's actual condition? The on-screen text was inscrutable, as the author was unknown and no footnotes or hyperlinks pointed to the background of the document.

It is obvious—or should be obvious—that information like this, no matter how attractive it may appear, is useless. More problematic are those pages whose authors *are* listed but are otherwise unfamiliar to you. Suppose my Ashanti Gold site had included an author's name, with no supporting material as to his or her position, location, or relationship to the company. To follow up on this information, I need to put the Net to work. The first item on the agenda is to determine whether it is possible to reach the author through an electronic mail address; e-mail would allow me to ask questions about the accuracy of the material or to verify its source. An author who stands by his or her work should be willing to answer such questions.

An electronic mail address is the most basic clue to authorial experience and intentions; it allows you to probe more deeply into what the author has put on-line. It may be that you've stumbled across an excellent source published by an author who simply didn't realize that the necessary corroborative information is critical in your evaluations. And this is where the advantages of using the Net come into play. The ability to engage in a dialogue with the source of your material is largely unique to the Internet; let's face it, most of us don't write or call book or magazine article authors, no matter how impressed or enraged we are by what they wrote, whereas because electronic mail is fast, easy to use, and frequently answered, we send it.

Often on the Net you will see a hyperlink pointing to information about the author, or else an address that can be clicked upon to start your browser's mail function. Usually, authorial information is published at the bottom of a Web page, although the lack of standard-ization in page design means you can't rely on that location. Network navigation often means you simply must page through the various levels of hyperlinks until you've isolated the address of the pagemaker.

Using electronic mail for this purpose in no way violates any concept of Internet etiquette, provided the query is made in a nonjudgmental way. You don't want to imply that the author is presenting dubious information or to attack the design of his or her page; instead, the goal is to follow up on what you've seen posted and to know more about the source of the material. This gives the author the chance to do some-thing positive by realizing there is a gap in his or her page design and correcting it. A friendly note will often lead to further material as well, as the author can sometimes suggest other sites with information that might be valuable to you.

A more difficult question to answer is when you should use e-mail this way. In most situations, surfing the Net means reading Web pages and tunneling through their hyperlinks to other sites, often without extensive examination or study. If you employ Inter-net content as part of a broader package of informa-tion that includes other forms of media, including television, radio, newspapers, and books, then you will be able to weigh what you see on-line against what you see on the Web. It is only when you run across some-thing that is useful to you but hard to confirm through any other source that you should consider sending mail to the author. If you plan to cite the Web page in question in an article and need further confirmation about its accuracy, send mail. But be mindful of every-one's time, including your own, and don't send that message unless there is a genuine need.

Other Internet tools provide, or should provide, the same accessibility as Web pages. Messages on newsgroups or mailing lists are invariably accompanied by the author's address; in fact, it's considered good procedure in both media to direct particular questions to the author through mail rather than in the public forum. Those messages that could be read profitably by the entire group should be posted publicly; but suppose you want to follow up on something a writer has said and you know that the material would not flow with the ongoing discussion? That's a perfect time to send e-mail directly to the author for clarification or further facts, while not tying up the public debate.

And realize that authorship should not be construed in too narrow a sense. A site mounted by a research organization may possess powerful credibility even if some or all of its materials lack individual attribution. I am more than happy to cite information about the works of Rembrandt when my source is a Web page created by the National Gallery in Washington or the Rijksmuseum in Amsterdam. In such cases, I am confident in the skills of the source, knowing that what I find there will have passed the internal scrutiny of experts in the subject.

But suppose you want to learn more about the author or organization behind a Web site than you think is polite to ask? Is this person an authority in the field in question? Can he or she discuss the issues with confidence because of an educational background in the subject? Is the company actively involved in research in this field, or working on new materials that might be of interest? There is a way to find out that doesn't involve electronic mail, one that allows you to search deeply without the potential embarrassment of a pointed e-mail questionnaire. The vehicle: an on-line search engine.

Are They Who They Say They Are?

When the Internet was a text-based environment, one of the most significant tools for obtaining information about people was a program called finger. Material a particular person chose to make available about his or her activities and interests was placed on-line in the form of two files, one called .plan, the other .profile (the period and the lowercase initial letter are both UNIX conventions). If you knew the e-mail address of the person in question, you could ask to see these files by using the command **finger** *address*, as in finger jthompson@victoria.unc.edu. If the person was on-line at the time, the command would alert you to the fact, and would display the contents of the .plan and .profile files stored on the user's workstation, which was usually a networked computer running UNIX.

The Internet's graphical capabilities have not meant the end of finger information; it is still available, often in the form of text supplemented by graphics; many users, for example, now include a photograph of themselves in their files. At an increasing number of sites, administrators are adding so-called finger gateways to the World Wide Web that provide a forms-based interface; you enter a user's name and click on the Search button. To find such sites or to track down individual addresses, you can run a search using one of the search engines. Such a search will pull up other mentions of your target as well.

Finger information is, however, rapidly being supplanted by personal Web pages, in which individuals put the same kind of material they would have originally posted in their .profile and .plan files on-line, along with, perhaps, a photograph and other materials. I've found everything from a database of favorite recipes to interactive diagrams of a user's model train layout. A search under a person's name will uncover these pages, and now that commercial on-line services like CompuServe and America Online have given their customers the ability to set up free Web pages, you'll see more such backgrounders, offering you the chance to take the measure of an Internet poster.

The Web's rich linkages can also direct you to projects the author is involved in or articles he or she has written. Many professionals have begun to place supporting materials for their jobs on-line. Academics may provide a page showing not only their teaching schedule but also a list of publications, while computer scientists may provide links to a library of programming tools they have created. When you're trying to verify that an author is indeed an authority on a particular subject, nothing beats the ability to read other materials he or she has written on it and to link to reviews in related publications. A good search engine will find these archives and provide evidence as to the author's reliability.

And search engines are not limited to World Wide Web materials. Several of the more prominent search engines—AltaVista, InfoSeek, and DejaNews —offer extensive databases of newsgroup postings. Using them, you can read prior postings from an individual to whichever newsgroups he or she frequents. Even if the author doesn't use a Web page or offer an archive of published materials, you can still tap into these far more informal postings in the newsgroups. Reading material posted in a variety of settings over time is an excellent way to assess credibility, not unlike using your conversations with people to get to know them.

Background Check

Consider the difference between reading an article in a magazine at the newsstand and on the Internet. The magazine article has been edited for space considerations and undergone an editorial process that focuses on concision; no editor wants to take up space with anything that isn't necessary. Consequently, when an author's ideas require substantiation or could benefit from related highlights requiring more room than the magazine can supply, all the author can do is to refer to the other documents in a footnote.

The Internet, on the other hand, gives this same author the ability to produce the necessary background information by means of a hyperlink. The difference is one of degree. For instance, a tightly reasoned argument may still fail to persuade me if I read only the published version of a particular story. But when I can examine the author's research materials, I can draw my own conclusions, and perhaps even find ideas I would not otherwise have been able to uncover. This method works particularly well in the academic arena, where scholarly journals are increasingly coming on-line. The ability to archive both the article and its surrounding web of research materials brings a new category of supporting documentation into play.

Consider a site called Into the Matrix: Your Filter to Cyberspace. The person behind this page is David S. Bennahum, a New York–based writer whose topic is the development of cyberspace. His site (http: //www.reach.com/matrix/welcome.html) is specifically directed at "exploring how technology and social change fuel each other." I learned about Bennahum from two sources, the first a mailing list Bennahum edits called MEME, the second a link he established on the Into the Matrix page itself which led to personal information and enough background to confirm his credentials as an Internet authority.

Bennahum's mailing list is actually an on-line newsletter that discusses technology issues on a bi-weekly basis. The MEME archive established at Bennahum's site gives access to back issues, as well as the current issue, while the interviews that comprise much of the material in MEME are presented in their full, unedited form through a separate hyperlink. Intrigued by what Robert Reich said to Bennahum about the power of technology to transform economies, I can read the complete interview here. I can also read questions and answers that have come in responding to the various issues of MEME—material that, once again, doesn't make it into the regularly distributed mailing for reasons of space and concision. Bennahum likewise includes the full text of articles he has written for such markets as *The New York Times*, *The Economist*, *Wired*, and *Harper's Bazaar*.

Breaking the Data Banks

If the Web can lead you to background materials on an author, an author's e-mail address (or, for that matter, a company name) can yield clues about related materials. Assume, for example, that you run across an interesting message on a mailing list from a person who seems to know a great deal about the wines of the Rhone Valley. You notice the poster's address:

dbl@bacchus.epicurious.com. You'd like more information about how to find good values in French wine, but you'd prefer to find it yourself rather than by sending e-mail to this person. With a little ingenuity, you can use the address to uncover an underlying Web site, even if you don't know that Epicurious Food is a business offering articles, recipes, and advertisements for consumers of fine wines and foods.

How? Most Web sites put a prefix of www in their address (the formula isn't invariable, but it occurs often enough that in most cases companies and other organizations will use it). On the chance that the poster of the message that interests you is connected to a Web site, you simply take his or her address and add a www prefix. The hypothetical address would thus be: www.epicurious.com. If you try to access this site with your browser, you will soon find yourself looking at a directory of wine and food features that includes, among such tantalizing offerings as recipe databases for *Gourmet* and *Bon Appétit*, a forum for wine lovers, a set of vintage reports from experts, and an on-line guide to building a good cellar for less than $500.

Again, the formula is to take the domain name that identifies the company or organization and plug it into the basic Web address. Thus an e-mail address of jackr@poobah.slipcase.com might become www.slipcase.com (note to use only the top-level domains in this formula, as the name immediately after the @ symbol refers to a computer at the site where the addressee receives his or her mail). Then enter the site in your Web browser and see if it leads to anything. You'll frequently be surprised at what you find; this method often uncovers companies whose existence you may have been unaware of, which may specialize in precisely the area you want to investigate. In my own work, it has led to the discovery of on-line journals and research organizations I had not found by using the search engines I usually consult.

What's in a Name?

One important thing to know about Internet addressing is that it requires you to follow the conventions of the Domain Name System. Like the format we use to direct letters through "snail mail," Internet addresses must take a particular form. An address that ends with the suffix org, for example, signifies an organization; the address might look like this: info@hrcb. org. In this case, the reference is to an organization whose name probably involves four words that are used to form the apparent abbreviation. Commercial enterprises use com as their suffix; addresses ending in edu point to educational institutions.

Internet addresses are always read from left to right, going from the most specific to the most general, just like snail-mail addresses. Thus, in the address george@cerulean.multinet.com, george is the user name of the person receiving mail at this address. He receives that mail on a computer called cerulean, which is in turn a part of something called multinet; all we know about the latter is that it is a commercial firm, as shown by the com at the end of the address. The address contains several subdomains, but the one to the far right is called the top-level domain; it will usually tell you something useful about the site.

This information can be helpful in the absence of other links to sources. Let's say you're planning to purchase a new VCR, but want to do some research so that this time you bring one home that you *can* program. You decide to use your burgeoning Internet skills to access information on this topic. Using the Domain Name System as your guide, you would, for example, evaluate a message about VCRs differently depending on its source. If it came from john_smith@samsung.com, you might infer you were dealing with someone connected to the Korean manufacturer Samsung (although even here you must be careful, for domain names like these have been assigned largely on a first-come, first-served basis, meaning that another company could be using this address). You would probably take at face value Mr. Smith's descriptions or price information about the VCR models made by Samsung, knowing that the information came from the company itself. But what if he posted a long message reviewing one of these machines? I would be skeptical of a glowing review of a VCR that was written by what might be one of the company's marketers, just as I would question reviews posted on the manufacturer's Web site if the documents were not fully attributed to independent authors and publications.

Aiming a critical eye at addresses can be helpful in a variety of ways. If I were reading a message about the increase in tuition at major universities and saw that the poster's address was john_smith@umsl.edu, I would at least know I was dealing with someone at an academic institution, whether faculty or student. Such information helps us collect clues so we can make an informed judgment about what we read. A message on Internet history from hal_johnson@isoc.org comes from someone at a nonprofit organization (thus the org suffix). We can surmise little from this, however, unless we also learn that isoc stands for The Internet Society, the umbrella organization that promotes the creation and maintenance of Internet standards. No one can learn every Net abbreviation, of course, but as your experience grows, you will learn to read these addresses to gain insight into the possible motives of their owners.

The increasing internationalization of the Internet has also made the implementation of country-level domains necessary, and each country on the Internet now has a two-letter identifier. The country domain name for the United States is us, although it is not used frequently. But once you leave the United States, country identifiers are used extensively. While both geographical and organizational domains are in use, no real confusion arises because both types are recognized throughout the world.

How useful are country domains for your content evaluation? Consider when you might want to know the country of origin of a particular poster of information. On the newsgroup soc.culture.celtic, you stumble across a discussion of Sinn Fein that goes into considerable depth about the political organization that makes it run. When you examine the poster's address, you find the ie suffix that identifies the Republic of Ireland. That alone is not enough to ensure that the information is correct, but it does give the sender more authority, and also more involvement, than a similar posting from, say, Canada.

You have to think on your feet when you evaluate a network address. The Internet is not a world of absolutes, but rather one in which judgment calls about information are common, and you must sift carefully through the various possibilities looking for reliability and veracity. Consider the address bljones@ amnesty.org. The org domain is for nonprofit corporations, so we don't necessarily assume a commercial motive in any postings originating from this person (or perhaps it's better to say, we're just less suspicious about the issue). The name amnesty catches our eye. Is this Amnesty International? As always, avoid jumping to conclusions. When an issue is important, either send e-mail to the person in question or try a Web site address, using the methods described.

Web addresses should be analyzed as carefully as their electronic mail equivalents. Consider the Web address www.pizzahut.com. This is the Pizza Hut Web site, with sample menus and ordering information. You can see by examining the address that the company identification is obvious. While we can't verify that it is Pizza Hut until we actually examine the page, the com domain verifies that we are dealing with a commercial site. A check with our Web browser confirms the company's identity.

Another address, www.pc.ibm.com/thinkpad/index.html, is likewise commercial, as shown by the com domain. The address implies that we are dealing with IBM, as a pass at the site with our browser will verify; the address also implies that the site is devoted to personal-computer issues, as shown by the pc in its address. This is a site devoted to IBM ThinkPad computers, the company's portable machines, and the page we are going to find at this address is an index of the information about those machines.

More complex is the address vishnu.nirvana.phys. psu.edu/argentina/argentina.html. Note that there is no www prefix; as mentioned, not all Web pages use it. The home page in question is an attempt to collect all available Internet information about Argentina, with hyperlinks to the various sources. But the country prefix for Argentina, ar, is nowhere in sight. Instead, we simply see an edu domain, indicating an educational institution. A check at the site reveals that the material here is written entirely in Spanish; but the home page also announces that the page is maintained by a woman named Elena Fraboschi, who lists her own e-mail address at the University of Indiana. A second server with a German address (the domain is de) is likewise listed as a source.

Confused? Remember that the World Wide Web can connect a single home page to multiple computers all around the world, and it's also possible to set up mirror sites, in which files are duplicated on other computers as well. As you examine such a site, you must decide for yourself how authoritative its information is. Don't assume that what you receive is necessarily true because it comes from the country that is the subject of the information. And don't assume that it necessarily is located in that country. In the case of the Argentina server, we are dealing with one of the most informative single-country sites on the Internet, but it takes a trip to the site to make that determination.

What about the address home.aol.com/joedk329/? AOL stands for America Online. AOL, like competitors CompuServe and Prodigy, has begun offering full Internet access to its members. As part of its service, members can create their own home pages at no charge. Moreover, AOL makes these home pages accessible both to members and to nonmembers using the Internet with a search engine. If you run into a Web page with an address that shows a commercial information service as the network behind it, consider the cost of posting the information. We do this all the time at the newsstand. There, a free publication is generally one that is supported entirely by advertising. How do you evaluate its content? Within the context of common sense. It could be that such a publication contains the work of the next Hemingway, but the odds for finding serious, high-quality content are higher when you pay your money for a magazine that makes enough money to pay its writers well. In Web terms, if it costs someone a monthly fee to maintain a site on-line, then that person is clearly motivated to be on-line. And while motivation hardly equates to quality, the adage that you get what you pay for hasn't survived all these years by chance. This is not an attack on free information or the people who post it—after all, those of us who use flat-rate Internet accounts spend a great deal of time posting and exchanging ideas. It does suggest that the lower the cost of posting, the more likely you are to encounter those with only a casual interest in their publications.

The On-Line Dotted Line

While the World Wide Web makes it relatively easy to link to background information about the author of a document, the newsgroups are more challenging. The typical newsgroup posting does include an author's e-mail address; in fact, readers often use electronic mail to continue discussions started in the newsgroup. We can therefore follow up what an author has said with questions of our own, either public or private.

But equally useful in the newsgroups are the so-called signature files that are commonly appended to postings. A signature is generally a statement of the poster's name, position, address, and frequently a favorite quotation. It may be simple or complex, although lengthy signature files are frowned upon by experienced hands since they take up needless bandwidth. Here, for example, is a (fictitious) signature of the sort that can provide helpful background information about the author of a message:

```
----------------------------------------------------------
John H. Rodriguez            johnr@apollo.controls.com
President, Continental Controls, Inc.
Inertial navigation systems for the space industry
"If you can launch it, we can track it."
----------------------------------------------------------
```

Suppose you have been reading a newsgroup discussion about the Challenger disaster. One poster claims that the government knew where the various parts of the space shuttle fell after the 1986 explosion that killed its crew; this poster is adamant in believing that NASA slowed the search for debris deliberately to calm public furor after the incident. But a response from Mr. Rodriguez outlines a different view: that the tracking systems following Challenger on its liftoff could only provide a general indication of the ocean area into which it fell. His reply seems authoritative, but it's the signature that could clinch his believability, for it tells you that this is a man whose job description involves him with the very systems examined in the discussion.

Signature files appear not only in newsgroups but also in mailing list messages and electronic mail. Users normally configure their software so that the signature is posted automatically at the end of any message they send. Considering that a carefully worded signature file can establish credentials in a debate, your own signature should reflect your background and expertise. Signature files will frequently be your only source of information and, conversely, your only statement of reliability, for on-line postings.

The Audience

Newsgroup and mail programs allow you to send copies of any message to one or more additional recipients using the aptly named carbon copy feature. As a researcher, you can use this information to learn more about the poster of a given message. Checking this carbon copy data offers an idea of the kind of audience this person considers ideal for his or her message, which can, in turn, tell you something about the intentions behind it.

Identifying the other recipients of an e-mail message of a newsgroup posting is not difficult. For example, I recently ran across a controversial message in the alt.wired newsgroup that involved U.S. federal government policy toward the Internet and, more broadly, what is called the National Information Infrastructure. The message denounced several people who are prominent in the government's efforts to extend electronic networking into K–12 schools across the United States. By looking at what was listed under the heading Newsgroups on the message's header, I learned that the posting had also been sent to a newsgroup focusing on the issues surrounding privacy and the rights of individuals in cyberspace, as well as government policy affecting same; to a newsgroup that focuses on computers and their impact upon society; to a newsgroup discussing legal issues of all kinds; to a group that considers issues of intellectual property; and finally, to a newsgroup devoted to journalistic questions, including how the Internet is playing an increasing role in the way news is distributed and read.

The carbon copy information reveals that the intent of the original message is serious. The population of any newsgroup varies greatly, but people sub-scribing to a group like comp.org.cpsr.talk, which focuses on computers and their societal impact and is sponsored by Computer Professionals for Social Responsibility, are not likely to be engaging in idle chatter. Experience is the key in this endeavor; as your expertise on the newsgroups increases, you will learn that each has its own tone and content, ranging from the frivolous to the scholarly. If in doubt, sub-scribe to the carbon-copied groups for a day or two to observe the tenor of the conversations there.

Suppose you run across a posting that makes a seemingly coherent argument for reexamining Ein-stein's theory of relativity. Perhaps you can't tell much about the poster from the e-mail address or the sig-nature, but the carbon copy list indicates that this per-son has sent the same message to these newsgroups: alt.nocturnal.ufo, alt.paranet.ufo, alt.conspiracy, and alt.consciousness.mysticism. What would you con-clude? The fact that the poster has an interest in un-identified flying objects, conspiracy theories, and mysticism doesn't, ipso facto, mean that his or her ideas are tainted. But it does tell you that this is the intellectual milieu within which those ideas are flour-ishing, and thus provides some clues as to how seri-ously you should take the posting. You could examine the discussions in these newsgroups to determine for yourself the quality of the debate there.

A group called talk.politics.guns is clearly a forum for proponents and opponents of gun control. A mes-sage cross-posted to it might indicate that its poster is someone with a fervent interest in that issue, but it should also remind you that hot topics—gun control, abortion, and the like—are likely to inspire more emotion than fact.

But how do you know what complicated names like comp.org.eff.talk refer to in the first place? To begin with, the newsgroups are divided into basic hierarchies. As with addresses, these are read left to right. Thus, the comp.org.eff.talk newsgroup can be broken out this way: The top-level hierarchy is comp, which is a category of newsgroups that focus on computing issues, from the philosophy of networking computers to the nuts and bolts of specific hardware; the org category directly below it tells us we are dealing with an organization, whose name—Electronic Frontier Foundation—is abbreviated to its initials in the next category, eff; the talk statement at the end tells us that this is where we will find discussions about issues important to the organization. A related newsgroup is comp.org.eff.news, which posts news items of interest to members. Needless to say, with tens of thousands of newsgroups available on the Internet, learning what all their acronyms stand for is not something you can accomplish in a day. In some cases, as in groups like alt.consciousness. mysticism, the meaning will be clear. In others, as in alt.business.multilevel.exceltel, it will be difficult to determine unless you sign on to the newsgroup and read some of its postings.

Asking the Right Questions

A typical beginner mistake on both newsgroups and mailing lists is to join and immediately post a message asking for broad information about a topic. Longtime subscribers grow weary of seeing the same obvious and oft-answered questions go through their computers when the answers to such inquiries are available in a Frequently Asked Questions document, or FAQ.

A FAQ is a listing of the most obvious questions that concern the subject of the newsgroup or mailing list. If you're joining a newsgroup to learn more about a topic, keep your eyes out for the FAQ document, which will often appear on a regular basis as a posting to that group. You can also join the newsgroup news.answers, which collects FAQs from all the newsgroups and posts them as they arrive. A few minutes spent with a FAQ will answer the primary questions, and FAQs are frequently updated. The use of a FAQ can fill you in on information you need to interpret particular postings.

Which brings us to the issue of etiquette. Unfortunately, along with the genuine help newsgroups and mailing lists can provide, there are instances of abuse, such as entire school classes being urged by their teachers to post messages on mailing lists asking for help with their homework. In one college course, a class was directed to use a mailing list on ecology as a resource; the specialists on the list, most of them scientists, found themselves coping with a sudden influx of beginner questions, jeopardizing the ongoing debate.[2]

Mailing lists and newsgroups can indeed serve as resources, but users should always consider the nature of the discussion before venturing forth: Is it made up of a small group of academic specialists who are used to working on collaborative projects, or is it more general in nature? What is its tone? Who are its main contributors, and what are their backgrounds? You can learn all this by spending time reading the list or newsgroup before you even consider posting to it. And if you do post, be advised that mailing lists and newsgroups, by their nature, take time to produce results. No one has time to read every message daily; in some cases, the message you post today won't be read for weeks. Patience is often rewarded with good information, while jumping back on the mailing list and demanding an immediate response is a sure way to lose credibility.

Analyzing Web Pages

Updates are serious business in the information game. You wouldn't make a presentation on your company's growth in the marketplace using numbers that were out of date, nor would you want to quote someone whose views had changed crucially in the three years since the publication you're referencing appeared. The point? Always look for date information in the Web pages you examine. A good page designer will be sure to include update information as part of each home page. If you can't find it and the material in question is important, send e-mail to the site to ask about dates.

Seems simple enough, but dates on-line are more complex. It is necessary to distinguish between three kinds of dates. First, when was the item produced? Second, when did it actually appear on the Web page? And finally, when was it last revised? A well-managed site will include information about all these, but of the three, the first is the most significant; it tells you about the currency of the information in question. Without it, you can form no judgment about the document's validity.

Be advised that good software gives you ways to view data that aren't immediately obvious. Suppose, for example, that you're reading material on a Web page and want to know more about the article you've retrieved. You can ask your browser to present any background information that's available. In Netscape Navigator, for example, you would pull down the View menu and look for an item marked Document Info, which tells you where the file is stored and provides an update on when it was last modified. It also tells you what type of file you are examining and offers a variety of other data. Other Web browsers perform the same functions in their own way.

The links on a particular Web page are also useful indicators; they tell you what related information may be available on remote computers and provide a clue to the reliability of the page in front of you. A page on modern art that offers links to major museum exhibits is one that is using the Web's potential to create nested information to its fullest potential. You can evaluate links on the basis of how comprehensive they seem to be: Do they offer a mere sampling of what's available, or do they attempt to cover the subject in detail? A site that also evaluates its links to remote computers in some way is helpful; such ratings can save you time as you investigate. The best sites will create a balance between outward-pointing links and their own materials.

You should also judge Web pages in terms of their comprehensiveness. Certainly, Web-based materials are now the most common sources of information on the Internet, but don't overlook the still-significant holdings at FTP and Gopher sites, particularly outside the United States and Western Europe. Depending on your subject, a Web page that ignores this universe of documents and files could be providing you with only a partial look at your subject. It's as easy for a Web browser to access an FTP directory or a Gopher menu as a Web page, so you should expect a comprehensive site to include links to any such relevant resources.

Stability of information is also a key issue. A reliable Web site will be one that keeps its links active, that is to say, ensures that its links still lead somewhere. This is easier said than done, because Internet sites are in a state of constant flux, so that a link to a particular Web page may quickly become obsolete when the administrator at a remote site decides to make a change in the directory structure there. If the page you are examining is carefully maintained, however, you will find few, if any, links that no longer function. If your experience of a Web page is that numerous links are dead ends, view the site with suspicion.

Hearing and Viewing Multimedia

Of course, the best World Wide Web sites are those that take advantage of digital media to provide new content rather than merely reflecting the old. Such sites expand the capabilities of broadcast media by providing video and audio on demand. Envision a future in which hearing your favorite radio show or watching a particular television segment is done at the time of your choice through content shipped over the Net.

Time magazine is a good example. Using its site (http://pathfinder.com/), you can not only read the text available in the print publication but can also view photographs not available in the print version. Thus, an on-line story on politics could be sprinkled with sound files from the candidate or his or her opponents. Obviously, such materials can provide you with a kind of information not obtained through text. Marks of strain in a voice, the sound of exhaustion or exhilaration in a speech—these things provide clues to the candidate and his or her beliefs. And a technique called *streaming audio* enables us to download and listen to a radio show in real time, so we can use the Internet as a digital archive for such shows (previously, audio materials like this had to be laboriously downloaded and then played back from disk).

Audio on demand over networked computers is a fascinating concept. It is one area where Internet content presents a genuinely different take on examining information. Normally, you have to be within earshot of a radio receiver to hear a particular show, and you need to be there when that show is airing. To be sure, a tape recorder also allows you to time-shift by playing the show whenever you please, but you have to know what you want to record and when it airs to capture it. By putting audio on the Internet, the possibility opens for searchable archives of such interviews and other content. Suppose a fellow fan of William Gibson, the science fiction author, tells you about an interview Gibson gave to the Canadian Broadcasting System in 1995. Using an audio player, you can access this interview as part of your research into Gibson's effect on science fiction. Increases in network bandwidth will soon make streaming video an equally malleable resource, although the technology is still in its experimental stages, awaiting the development of superior-quality images.

How do you evaluate such materials? As with any other Internet content, the primary task is to examine the source. In the case of the Gibson interview, the first questions to ask are who set up and recorded the original interview, and when was it done? After using a search engine, I found the interview on the RealAudio World Wide Web site, where links to various kinds of audio sources are given. By following the links, I could venture to a listing of the interviews available and the source radio networks. Any audio site worth considering will be specific about the sources of its content and supporting information; after all, the reason you want to access a particular item, whether text, video, or audio, is that it provides something worthwhile.

Case Studies in Content Evaluation

How you think critically on-line is dependent on context. Each Web site, each newsgroup posting, each mailing list message, presents its own potential points of confirmation or rejection; the skills of its writer and/or designer influence significantly the judgment you must make, and provide the supporting envelope of evidence. Here are five scenarios, some of them fictitious, some of them real, against which to apply the tools of on-line evaluation.

A student at the University of Maryland is troubled to hear that a woman living nearby has been abusing her daughter. He uses on-line newsgroups to voice his concerns, posting messages in discussion areas concerned with psychology, politics, and child welfare. The messages list the woman's telephone number and urge readers to call the woman ". . . and tell her you are disgusted and you demand she stops."[3] As a result, the woman receives a number of harassing calls from newsgroup readers. If you read such a message, how seriously should you take it? Should you call?

In Bath, England, a man named Keith Hudson is constructing what may be the first Internet university through an organization called InterSkills. The group's World Wide Web site contains documents that support Hudson's theories; namely, that the university system has been superseded, as have many of the economic institutions that surround it. Hudson sees technologies like the Internet as leading to the rebirth of strong local economies, resembling those that flourished in the early Middle Ages. He also believes that computer-assisted learning spells the end of teaching as we know it, particularly in the humanities. If you visit the InterSkills site, how much credence should you give to the arguments it marshals about education and the economy? How would you use the Internet itself to draw your conclusion?

You're planning a trip to Costa Rica and have located an on-line document that provides a listing of hotels in San José, along with seemingly useful information on currency exchange rates and the local economy. The material is just what you need, but it contains no reference to its author or when it was written. How can you find out when the article was last updated, and who wrote it? And can you generate related information about Costa Rica that will help you evaluate its key premises?

An electronic archive of research papers has been established to provide physicists with access to the work of their colleagues in fields like astrophysics, condensed matter, superconductivity, and materials theory. Subscribers receive title, author, and abstract information as new papers arrive, and they can retrieve the full article if it interests them. The site is funded partially through the National Science Foundation. If you access an article abstract here, how do you put it in the context of other information in the field, and how does it compare to traditional print forms of distribution?

On an Internet mailing list, you sit in on a discussion about television violence. On one side is a man who argues that the number of violent acts on television is directly correlated to the rise in homicides in America's inner cities. On the other is a woman who insists that studies have proven that what people see on television has no bearing on what they are likely to do in real life. A third person claims that the television networks are making contingency plans to scrap all violent programming in prime time as a result of governmental pressure. How can you determine which of these three, if any, is the most reliable? How can you dig out further material on this topic?

The Maryland case tells us much about the Internet in miniature, even as it reminds us that the types of content differ according to their posting mechanism, each of which presents its own set of demands. Newsgroups are generally unmoderated, which means that no one exerts any control over their content. If someone wants to post a message, that message will appear, and will in turn be read by anyone who follows the newsgroup on a regular basis. The only correction for a bogus message, then, is the posting of a follow-up message that calls into question what was said in the earlier post. This self-corrective dialogue (multilogue?) often leads to a series of increasingly acrimonious exchanges; in their most antagonistic form, they're referred to as *flames*.

In the Maryland case, we are looking at information posted by an individual concerned about someone else's welfare. As in everyday life, we have to decide how trustworthy the individual is before we know how to evaluate the message. How, for example, would you size up the same message if it were posted on the bulletin board in your neighborhood laundromat? What if it came in the mail as an anonymous note?

A glance at any signature file at the end of the posting may provide us with clues about the sender; this message would be more significant if it came from someone involved in social welfare work than from a concerned college student. We can also look at the electronic mail address to see if we can ferret out any clues about the poster that way. Is the domain an educational (edu) site or a company (com)?

A search engine is the next recourse as we try to learn more. By searching a database of newsgroup postings; we can learn to which other groups a person has posted in the past. This sets up an oblique judgment about reliability. If the poster in question (in this case, the university student) turns out to be a frequent participant in newsgroups focusing on soap operas, we might infer that he has an obsessive interest in other people's lives. We might then read some of those earlier postings to see what issues concern him, deciding from their tone and style whether he seems reliable. If the answer still isn't obvious, we could do one of two things: Run a search for World Wide Web pages under his name, looking for a possible home page he maintains; or send him electronic mail asking him for evidence to back up his charges. The key point is that newsgroup postings are your least likely sources of substantiated information, given their freewheeling nature. Unless you're willing to go through this kind of difficulty to verify a posting, you shouldn't act on its urgings.

The second case is an example of on-line publication in service to an idea, a format at which the Internet excels. InterSkills is a relatively scholarly site devoted to exploring a controversial model for economics (http://www.on-the-net.com/interskills/); its key components are the various support materials chosen to strengthen its case. Although it's well designed and convincing, we need to find ways to learn more about its ideas from external sources. Hyperlinks to other sites are one solution; we can get a feel for what people interested in similar areas think of the InterSkills approach by following the links it has established on its page. Another possibility is to examine the author (in this case, Keith Hudson). We can run keywords from the site, including the author's name, through a search engine to look for material that will support or cast doubt upon his conclusions. At this point, we're trying to unearth reviews, both pro and con, that aren't hyperlinked off the InterSkills page itself, and thus might be more impartial in their evaluation.

Here the ability to analyze a Web page becomes paramount. We should study the site to learn when the material on it was created, mounted on the server, and updated. An examination of the site's various links will also tell us whether it is being maintained on a regular basis, which in turn will either lend credence or cast doubt upon the viability of the project. We should also examine any archival materials made available here, looking for the focus of the information (is it scholarly or popular in nature?), its currency, its style, and the degree to which it is supported by references. Hyperlinks leading to the author's own writings would be useful; if they exist, we can contrast his views with any materials we generate through hyperlinks to related sites and comments about his work.

The third case (your planned trip to Costa Rica) comes from a less theoretically oriented Web site.

Exchange rates are matters of hard numbers; the material is either right or wrong, and can be verified in a bank or by a call to the public library. But what about the other information about Costa Rica, which you'd likewise want to use? A first step is to check on the data to learn when it was posted and last updated. You may then want to contact the site by e-mail to learn who wrote the Costa Rica materials, thus forming a judgment on how reliable the information is. A search engine can turn up other postings by this author either on the Web or in the newsgroups, while hyperlinks on the Costa Rica page may provide materials posted on other sites against which to measure the page in question. You may want to ask questions of a larger audience as well; your own posting on a travel-related newsgroup may uncover comments from other users of the Costa Rica site, as well as revealing further sources of information about your trip. The key above all is to compare and contrast this data with established sources, on or off the Net, before committing your own time and money on the basis of what you find at one location.

The fourth case (archived physics research papers) is an example of an already established research mechanism migrating from the print medium onto the Internet. Here the question is immediately clarified by a trip to the site (http://xxx.lanl.gov/). Given the credentials of its participants, its backing by government agencies, and its clear links to publications with a distinguished history, we know that we are dealing with edited content that has undergone a peer review process. The site is specialized and comprehensive; browsing through it will confirm that its material is kept up to date through frequent editing and that its links are sound. Any suspicion that might remain can be quickly assuaged by running a search, either through a Web search engine or one specializing in the newsgroups. The remarks of scholars who have used the site serve as a powerful assurance that it is reliable, as do articles in which this resource is favorably reviewed.

Finally, what do we do with an argument on a mailing list (in this case, a discussion on television violence)? We can use search engines to look for information about the participants as a starter. When controversial topics are debated, our first goal is to take the measure of the debaters; we can read any newsgroup postings they have made in the past, or scout for Web pages either maintained by them or mentioning them, including possible archives of articles they have written. We can also look at signature files at the end of their messages, determining whether any of them has a job description, for example, that gives particular credence to his or her views. Electronic mail addresses may uncover corporate affiliations. In the end, much of our judgment of this kind of discussion will come down to matters of style and supporting evidence. How well do the participants acquit themselves in the argument, how carefully do they marshal their facts, how convincingly do they use supporting evidence? The distinction between edited and unfiltered content remains paramount, which reminds us to check such things as media-oriented Web sites for their views.

Each of these situations presents a different set of challenges. For if there is one lesson the Internet teaches, it is that not all content issues can be resolved. In some cases, we remain unconvinced despite all our labors, having learned that facts and judgment intertwine just as uneasily on the Net as they do in everyday life. In other cases, an issue will snap together with satisfying finality and prove decisive in our work. You will see that critical thinking is a skill that suffuses the entire on-line experience; all the Internet competencies invariably draw on it. It is the power of reason, the convergence of rationality and experience, that is the basis for critical thinking and evaluation. "Reason lies between the spur and the bridle," as George Herbert once said, and the Internet competencies to which we now turn all depend upon good intellectual horsemanship.

CHAPTER

From Hypertext to Context

It's sometimes said that hypertext is nonlinear, mean-ing it frees us from the need to read through a docu-ment line by line so that we can jump about from one idea to another and thus open a unique route through the text. True enough, but the way we read has always offered this capability; what differed was the kind of book we were reading.

I'm writing this with a Dvořák symphony (the 6th) playing through the Internet via RealAudio, its win-dow out of view, the volume low enough so as not to be distracting. Microsoft Word is on my screen, and in spite of the peaceful background music, what I'm looking at worries me. In a third window on my screen is the Asia Inc. Online page, offering financial news and analysis from the Pacific Rim markets (http://www.asia-inc.com/). My own positions in Hong Kong have grown incrementally over the years, and for reasons like those shown on the Asia Inc. page. For example, an article by Chalmers Johnson, the president of the Japan Policy Research Institute, explains why the emergence of China will be the most critical business issue of the twenty-first century. A related article examines how China's increasing urbanization changes marketing strategies there.

Indeed, legions of writers, pundits, and fund managers have made the same bullish call on China, which is why so much investment capital has flowed into Hong Kong in recent years. After all, China takes over Hong Kong for good in 1997; a benign outcome there will benefit the entire region if the Chinese leadership allows the former colony's economic engines to continue turning over without undue restraint. The Asia Inc. page gives me the Hong Kong daily news summary, where I can check items affecting my investments in companies like Hopewell Holdings and Cheung Kong, while its technical commentary weighs the strengths of the Asian currencies. A major feature story hyperlinked here considers the case for Shanghai as Asia's next business megalopolis.

So why am I worried? Because of what I'm *not* seeing on this page. Other media sources—CNN, *The Economist, The New York Times*—tell me that among the Asian mergers and acquisitions, tensions have yet to be resolved about China's relationship with the United States, particularly as it relates to the infringement of intellectual rights covering CDs and computer software. That subtext bubbles fitfully beneath the surface chatter about economic growth, affecting other stocks I own, like Boeing, whose sales in China are hurt by political uncertainty. Taiwan continues to be an issue: Would China dare invade the island? Nor is T'ienanmen Square a distant memory, leaving me to wonder in whose hands I'm putting so much of my capital. And what about the sweatshops, where women and even young children are exploited for the sake of cheap exports?

These questions intertwine in the fugal play of business, and I'm concerned that I don't see hyperlinks to any of them on my screen. Therein the point: As with any other form of media, what you see online must be weighed against its source. Asia Inc. would not necessarily be expected to highlight the more negative aspects of doing business in China, because that is not its charter. The site is run by *Asia Inc.*, a magazine that lists its editorial mission as " . . . to tell the extraordinary story of Asia's top executives and their enterprises in their own words and images, and to serve in this manner as the voice of Asian business as it prepares for the Pacific Century." The magazine and its Web page are pro-Asia, and their stance is clearly reflected in how they have built their site.

This is the paradox of hypertext—it establishes links to banks of information, leading to the assumption that ideas are always backed by evidence. And a hypertext discussion can be *manipulated* by the choice of those links. What appear to be inevitable connections to related facts are actually *choices* made by page designers whose views are reflected in their selection of links. As much as we are dealing with a new medium, we are nonetheless forced back upon older and more familiar critical judgments involving the source of information and its involvement in the story.

Hyperlinks: Guidance or Manipulation?

Hyperlinks are shown through underlining and color changes; most browsers highlight the links to related content in blue. The reader sees text with certain elements clearly labeled as significant; these are the ones to which the eye is drawn, while other words and phrases lose emphasis because they are not selected for linkage. In a similar fashion, a newspaper can, by its choice of subheads and placement of stories on a page, determine your perception of the importance of a particular news item. It's important to keep this framework in mind as you read. Appropriate questions to ask of all Web content are: What should I be seeing here that I am not? Is there another side to this issue that's not being presented?

I could, for example, present the news about China in entirely different ways than Asia Inc. Imagine a portion of my earlier paragraph, now set up as a hyperlinked Web page: "Other media sources—CNN, The Economist, The New York Times—tell me that among the Asian mergers and acquisitions, tensions have yet to be resolved about China's relationship with the United States, particularly as it relates to the infringement of intellectual rights covering CDs and computer software. That subtext bubbles fitfully beneath the surface chatter about economic growth, affecting other stocks I own, like Boeing, whose sales in China are hurt by political uncertainty. Taiwan continues to be an issue: Would China dare invade the island? Nor is T'ienanmen Square a distant memory, leaving me to wonder in whose hands I'm putting so much of my capital. And what about the sweatshops, where women and even young children are exploited for the sake of cheap exports?"

This paragraph acts as a set of pointers, but the choice of hyperlinks (shown by underlining) says everything about my viewpoint. If you wanted to learn more about the broad term *sweatshops*, for example, you could put your cursor over it in this hypothetical hypertext document, clicking to be whisked to, perhaps, a news account of abuses in a textile factory. A click on T'ienanmen Square might take you to a video about the brutal crackdown that ended (temporarily, at least) the democracy movement in China, while my link to CNN might provide a less than flattering story about censorship in that country. Clearly, a page constructed with these kind of links is making a different rhetorical statement about China's economy than one like Asia Inc.'s, which is filled with hyperlinks to stock market tables and corporate profiles. Both appear to forge necessary connections to the background information supporting their particular positions; both leave out links to information that calls that position into doubt.

The point is, your view of hypertext should be considerably different from your experience of the printed page. When you read text in book or newspaper, the only visual emphasis is the occasional use of bold or italics, or the clear marking of a chapter head. Good writing rarely requires additional emphasis; it should present its ideas in such a way that the reader understands where the weight of the paragraph falls, and knows how to interpret the focus of a sentence. Accenting these things with too promiscuous a use of italics and bolding is thus a kind of copout, an easy way to make points without building the requisite rhetorical skills.

Hypertext puts emphasis back into the text by turning certain words and phrases blue and underlining them. These emphases are determined by a programmer with a hypertext editor who creates hyperlinks in specific places. Thus we see hypertext emerging as a new kind of rhetorical tool. Rhetoric considers the question of how to use media to influence the judgment or the emotions of the intended audience. Style is part of this, as is design. Whenever we decide where we want to place a particular image on a World Wide Web page, we're engaging in a rhetorical exercise, speculating about the image's impact on the reader who is viewing that page. Whenever we choose the links that we deem significant enough to bear linkages, we make a similar judgment. Hence, rhetoric, being about persuasion, can succeed through means fair and foul; we can consider how to move an audience by appealing directly to their worst instincts, or we can shape an argument around principles of truth seeking.

Read through a typical home page and you will be taken along a route that has been determined for you by that page's creator. The question about hypertext that people fail to ask is, who creates the hyperlinks? Their very presence signals which ideas are important and which, by being unlinked, are not. The critical reader must note which is which, and ask whether these choices are authoritative or arbitrary. A range of possible actions exists for making such determinations, but the point is that hypertext as a reading medium is unusually sensitive to manipulation. It's far too easy for a page designer to neglect a key objection to a particular point simply by not hyperlinking anything to it; the alternative viewpoint is therefore never seen. For the unwary reader, the experience of reading hypertext is all too often a search for the next hyperlink and a quick exit.

A key component of digital literacy, then, is wariness. Sequential reading allows an author to build an argument, buttressing the case with examples and taking advantage of the arts of persuasion. Hypertextual reading puts the rhetorical arts into an odd tension; the reader, rather than the author, is the one who charts a course through the document. This being the case, the author of hypertext has to consider which routes the reader will be allowed to take. In doing so, he or she can lay out an argument through the omission or addition of particular items that support the point being made. If I create a hypertextual document about the Holocaust in which every link points to a site that supports people who think it never happened, I am creating a phony information path, but one that, by the number of its links to outside sources, looks authoritative. Blithely ignoring the testimony of survivors, of the soldiers who entered the concentration camps after their liberation, of the jurists at Nuremberg, I can show you only the dubious "scholarship" of those who deny that these events ever happened.

Compounding the Issue

Hypertext takes us into the realm of the compound document, made up of distinct components displayed as a single entity. This is not possible to do with printed books unless we're willing to cut and paste parts of pages into a separate volume. And if we did that, our compound document, composed of pages and illustrations from a variety of books, would be a static thing. Once we glued the various parts of it into place, it would be as immutable as any of the printed materials that went into it. Updating its pages or rearranging its images would require wholesale surgery and reassembly, like one of the collages we all built when we were young.

An electronic compound document is a different kind of publication. It combines media types; it's as accurate—and as misleading—to call it a document as it is to call it a broadcast or a presentation, for it combines aspects of all these things. Central to the concept of a networked compound document is the idea that it must contain pointers—the links—to the various components it will display on the screen. That the compound document can thus be composed of geographically dispersed materials yet displayed on a common page is a testament to how much the client/server model of computing has changed our access to information. The fact that we can then use hyperlinks to move to these remote sites and explore their holdings reinforces this view.

Hypertext, of course, is only one aspect of the World Wide Web. Browsing acknowledges the meshing of media that we call *multimedia,* of which textual information is but a single component. What is novel is the ability to connect everything from sound files to animation to moving video to textual documents within a single frame, a so-called page of information. We can do this because computers can digitize these forms of media; to a computer, a file is a file, so that we can connect to a movie clip with the same point-and-click techniques we use to access a text file. When we do this, we move beyond the bounds of pure hypertext into the realm of a far more facile beast called *hypermedia.* The underlying computer functions remain the same, but the kind of information we pull in with our browsers changes. For all practical purposes, in today's Web the terms *hypertext* and *hypermedia* have become synonymous, although we can always call upon the distinction between text and other forms of media when there is need to make a specific point.

But whether in the form of hypertext or hypermedia, there is no question that linked electronic information provides new options for tying ideas together. Consider how information is presented in conventional publishing. A scholarly publication, for example, might provide a wide variety of pointers to supporting documentation. The standard footnote would appear at the bottom of each referenced page, or the collection of notes could be preserved as endnotes at the back of the book. The volume would also include a bibliography, a table of contents, and an index. And that is about as far as a standard book can be pushed in terms of information linkages.[1]

Just as a printed book uses footnotes to carry additional information above and beyond that presented by the regular text, so a hypertext document can point to background information that supplements what we read on the first pass. But the footnote analogy is inadequate to convey what hypertext can do; it's only a partial explication of a more malleable tool. Consider what a footnote usually is. In most cases, the note is a reference; the author is telling us that we can look up his or her source in the book or magazine article listed there. Some footnotes are more discursive, containing the author's ideas about the subject, but the physical nature of the bound book requires a certain degree of circumspection. If footnotes become too large, they intimidate the reader and break up the sequential flow of text. Thus a paragraph-length footnote might prove useful, whereas a three-page footnote is merely cumbersome.

These constraints do not appear on the World Wide Web, which lets us link to documents or programs of any size, and in ways that allow readers to construct their own experience of the text. We do see examples of hyperlinks set up as pure footnotes, but usually when the form of the printed book is closely followed on-line, and the hyperlink drops us to a different position on the same (lengthy) Web page, where the footnote can be read quickly and then left behind as we return to the main document. Such footnoting is not common compared to other forms of Web linkage. Why? Footnoting is an internal process; it connects information created by the same author or at the same site through inward-pointing links. In the universe of the printed book, such internal footnoting is all there is. Linkages have to be internal because there is no way for a bound book to link itself dynamically to someone else's work. While a footnote can point to another book or article, it cannot take you into its pages.

More common practice on the Web is to link to an entire page of related information. This is an emphatically external process, one in which the footnote model is largely abandoned. This is a major distinction between hyperlinks and footnotes. If footnotes refer to ever more precise additions to a particular idea, most Web hyperlinks do exactly the opposite. They tend to open up hitherto unknown channels of exploration. Thus a mention of the seaport of Shanghai in the context of a particular economic analysis opens out to an encyclopedic Hong Kong–based site containing information about the Chinese economy, its industrial base, and its infrastructure.

Hyperlinks in this sense are open-ended. They can connect documents of equal stature, of any length. They are references that alert the reader to the presence of resources in a globally connected cyberspace. Advisory in nature, they likewise point (in most cases) to sites that the author of the current hypertext page has no control over. Whereas a footnote is written by the author of the book in which it appears, a hyperlink can refer to a Web page written by someone the author of the current page knows little about. A hyperlink implies no necessary endorsement of that page, either; it merely testifies that it exists and *might* be useful. Hypertext is the ultimate contextual tool.

These differences are significant. The print model provides the assurance that whatever judgments we have formed about the author of the text can be extended into the glossary, footnotes, and index of the book. Hypertext on the World Wide Web changes the model. If we are currently reading a Web page whose author is clearly intelligent and reasonable, we may assume that he or she will set up hyperlinks to sites that share this worldview. But we can't *assume* that the hyperlinks will take us to information that is equally useful or valid. Each reading of a hyperlinked Web page, then, requires us to judge anew whether we are in the hands of a reliable source. As opposed to a print volume, on which we can pass a judgment over the whole book, hypertext and hypermedia come at us in a series of related digital documents, each of which is discrete. Thus the novelty of hypertext: The user both reads and constructs the information.

Reading versus Browsing

We read books, but we browse the Web—browse in the specialized sense of moving back and forth between linked information. Browsing differs from the traditional reading experience because it is not a static thing. Every time you pick up a book from a library shelf, its content is the same since the last time you looked at it, unless you've happened upon a new edition. But you can't make a similar assumption about the Internet. Access the same site on two consecutive days and you might find different content, ranging from an entirely rewritten home page to a revised set of hyperlinks, each of which in turn might lead to its own revised pages. We are still finding out what the Internet will become, but the interactive model of continuously updating information is one that appeals to modernists. It suggests a lack of permanence, a cultural relativism free from static truth that resonates in a world defined by quantum mechanics and the perplexing laws of Einsteinian physics. The great danger is that such relativism will seduce us into dividing into myriad clusters of common interests—tiny, self-reinforcing communities that can shut themselves off from countervailing viewpoints and reinforce only their own dogma.

Because electronic networking speeds the process of retrieval dramatically, it highlights the differences between browsing and traditional reading. It's important to understand this difference, or you'll wonder whether books will disappear in the next few years (they won't), or why hypertext doesn't become the model for everything from novels to literary biographies (it can't). Although a common dream of computer visionaries is the creation of vast hypertext libraries of information eventually storing the corpus of human knowledge, we should consider what actually happens when we work our way through a hypertext document, for that model has ramifications on how we think, not to mention how we carry on important activities like science and learning.

Hypertext is language formatted to fit a screen and possessed of the ability to connect to other text or other forms of media. Computer screens, in turn, are difficult to read; even the best can do little more than parody a printed page, and they lack the convenience of the printed book or newspaper to be leafed through. Indeed, the hypertext page is similar in many ways to precodex documents; as with a papyrus roll, what you see on-screen must be read by "scrolling" through the document. If you need to skim the content just to get its general sense, if you're looking for ideas but don't know which will catch your eye, hypertext will disappoint you. The hypertext model affirms the distinction between reading and browsing—thus, they are both necessary literacies.

It helps to realize that hypertext is an evolutionary, not a revolutionary, concept. Changes in technology have always helped us find things we have stored in memory—the memory of the mind, then the memory of the book, and now the memory of the machine. The first hypertext was probably created around the sixth century A.D., when we began to realize that books with pages that turn (codices) could contain individual page numbers. That meant that if we wanted to find something, we could go back to it quickly. It also meant that we could create an index that told us the location of what we needed. Need to check when the local prelate was installed? A glance at an index could tell us in which part of the chronicle to look. Good indexes quickly proved that raw information could be made much more powerful through systems of reference that speeded up the retrieval process. Speed wasn't everything, but it helped.

Thus hypertext's roots go back to the dawn of the bound-book era, significantly predating the development of the printing press. One intriguing argument has it that the Talmud, that great collection of rabbinical commentary on the Hebrew Bible, is itself an example of hypertext at play, with marginal notes providing a useful cross-referencing function.[2] Equally ancient are the Indian epics the *Ramayana* and the *Mahabharata*, which include stories branching off from other stories in hypertextual fashion.[3] Dictionaries and encyclopedias also can be considered, in their own way, forms of hypertext.

Hypertext in the modern sense seems to have been first visualized by Vannevar Bush in his seminal article "As We May Think," which forecast in 1945 so many of technology's breakthroughs to come[4]; the first practical hypertext device was created by Doug Engelbart at the Stanford Research Institute. Today we can take tools like indexes and reengineer them so that they don't exist as a separate document per se, but as a whole series of interconnected documents. Rather than a single index, we can point to a collection of supporting digital material. Or we can set up a standard index with hyperlinks so that we can jump immediately to the page in question, thus saving time.

But hypertext is a mental process as well as a digital tool. It's sometimes said that hypertext is nonlinear, meaning that it frees us from the need to read through a document line by line, so we can jump about from one idea to another and thus open a unique route through the text. True enough, but the way we read has always offered this capability; what differed was the kind of book we were reading. With a textbook in traditional, bound format, I might use the index to jump back and forth between topics, or read chapters out of sequence to follow the threads of an idea. I certainly do this with computer manuals;

when learning a new operating system, for example, I never read consecutively, but hit subjects I need to understand as the occasion arises.

On the other hand, hypertext is suited only to particular kinds of reading experience. I'm reading Livy's history of Rome in my spare time. Hannibal has crossed the Alps and is pushing toward Rome; no general has yet been found who can stop him, and after the disastrous battle of Cannae, Rome's last army has been destroyed. Do I want to jump around in this text? Absolutely not; the text and its narrative flow demands my full attention. For the experience of story, hypertext isn't well suited; for the ability to perform research, it is useful as few tools have been. We have always had the ability to do either kind of reading. What the Internet has done through hypertext is to allow us to do one kind faster, and to consider pointers to ideas as live links to related information.[5]

The Spinning of the Web

But the limits of the medium are profound. To move digital information to allow on-screen formatting, photographs, diagrams, moving video, sound, and text to appear side by side, all within the narrow constraints of bandwidth, each of these things must be turned into data packets and shipped piecemeal across the network. The packets must be reconstructed at the destination and then translated back into things we can work with on a computer screen. The Net must do all this quickly enough that we, with our modernist impatience, don't become disenchanted and find something else to do with our time.

These are no small problems, and no small magic is required to solve them. In typical Internet fashion, they were originally addressed by scientists out of the need to continue a far different enterprise. The physics center called CERN, for Conseil Européen pour la Recherche Nucleaire (the European Laboratory for Particle Physics), near Geneva, is world famous for its work on the smallest building blocks of matter. This is the domain of supercolliders, where particles are accelerated to near light speed and crashed into each other to create spectacular clouds of atomic debris.

The scientists who study these microcosmic incidents needed to be able to keep up with the work of their colleagues around the world, which is how Tim Berners-Lee, a British-born physicist at the laboratory, came into the picture. The idea was that hypertext, sans images, sound, and other hypermedia add-ons, could be used to foster communications between researchers, allowing them to exchange documents and data as necessary. Berners-Lee proposed the project in March 1989, and the first Web software made its appearance in 1990, running on a NeXT computer at the CERN site.

The key development behind the Web was Berners-Lee's creation of HyperText Transport Protocol, or HTTP. A Web client, or browser program, selects a particular hyperlink in a document. The link is identifiable by underlining or display in a different color from the surrounding text. When the user clicks on the hyperlink, the Web client contacts the computer at the address specified by the link and asks for the particular document being requested. The server at the other end of the connection then sends this material to the client program, which displays it on the user's screen. The information sent could be textual or could contain other forms of media. The World Wide Web as we know it today is the sum total of these transactions, millions upon millions of them, as they move through the universe of networked computers.

The Web uses a computer language called Hyper-Text Markup Language (HTML)—that allows Web developers to design their pages and specify their hyperlinks, thus connecting Internet materials from files at FTP sites to Gopher menus to newsgroups, not to mention other Web pages. All this is done through the Universal Resource Locator, or URL, which can point to a particular resource no matter where it's located on the Internet. URLs compress address information into as small a space as possible. Although these "addresses" are clunky, hard to remember, and seemingly inscrutable, they tell us everything we need to know to find a particular item on the Internet. And that's no small feat, given that the Internet is composed of tens of thousands of computer networks operating off millions of separate computers and regularly traveled by tens of millions of people.

Remarkably, in a relatively short period of time, we're moving from an Internet that resembles an endless rummage sale to one that in striking ways resembles a library, thanks to URLs. At a rummage sale, you never know what you'll find, so you spend your time walking down aisles stuffed with odds and ends, occasionally running across something that catches your eye. In a library, you use the card catalog, or the electronic equivalent of it, to quickly find what you need. Like library catalog cards, URLs are pointers, so they make it possible to set up an Internet that is usefully indexed. They also let us combine Internet material, files of all kinds, into single pages of information. Take a file from this computer and another from that one; both can be displayed on the same World Wide Web page, for the HTML language can point to each.

The problem with hypermedia documents is that they're difficult to display. In the early days of the Web, to use a hypermedia-laden page meant downloading a file to display a graphic and calling up an external viewer to see the result. The image would appear in a separate on-screen window from the Internet session you were running to read the text. A sound file would similarly be called up through a third-party program. Each media type demanded its own player, and the result was more of a collage than a contiguous page of information. What was missing was organization, and what was needed was an appropriate software tool. Such an all-purpose viewer soon appeared in the form of a program called Mosaic.

Mosaic was developed at the National Center for Supercomputing Applications in Urbana-Champaign, Illinois, on the campus of the University of Illinois. The team that put it together, led by programmers Marc Andreessen and Eric Bina, conceived the key concept that would change the Internet into today's multimedia powerhouse. That concept was that all the resources pointed to through URLs could be displayed by a single software program, which would translate the data conveyed by HTTP into user-friendly pages. Hyperlinks would become obvious; they could be shown in blue, or underlined, or both. Text and graphics could be displayed simultaneously, while pull-down menus and mouse-driven commands could enable features like a bookmark list, where the URLs of frequently accessed pages could be stored. Annotations were possible, allowing users to write notes that could be kept on their own machines, supplementing what the Web sent over the Internet. Mosaic did for the World Wide Web what the Macintosh and Microsoft Windows did for desktop computers. It democratized the process.

It's probably not accurate to say that Mosaic launched the Internet boom that has continued unabated since 1993; after all, growth had been rapid even before this. Between January 1990 and June 1991, for example, the number of connected networks making up the Internet grew from 2,200 to 4,000, an indication that even in the text-based environment, people were becoming curious about what the network offered. Nevertheless, it seems safe to argue that without Mosaic, the widespread acceptance of the Internet by the public, and particularly its spread into the commercial world, simply would not have occurred. Doubtless it would have remained the kind of offbeat, if fascinating, tool that the commercial information services already provided in miniature, a place where modem users could work their way through the process of sending mail and downloading files, but one that would remain more or less intimidating to computer neophytes.

It was Mosaic that put the idea of the compound document firmly into the public consciousness. The Mosaic display of a well-designed Web site reminded home users of television, the medium with which they were most familiar. While a Web page didn't move, it did offer attractive graphics and the capability of at least downloading sound. Text appeared, enough to make it seem like the enterprise was content-laden, but it was pictures that made the Web so attractive to the average newcomer, because pictures aren't intimidating. The idea that you could click on a hyperlink rather than submit a command also had resonance; it promised a computer network "for the rest of us," as the commercials say, one without the hassles of deep study or classroom training.

The trend in Internet software development is to make it ever more television-like, combining its already powerful features with the live-picture model of the broadcast networks. If this seems ironic, consider that change is most likely to take deep root when it grows organically out of concepts people already understand. Thus the subsequent development of Java, a programming language created at Sun Microsystems, whose whole reason for being is to provide Web pages that are not static. Java works by downloading small applications, called *applets*, to your computer, which then run and create action on your browser's display. Static text suddenly acquires a moving logo. A ticker showing sports scores can now update itself. For the user, the effect is one of linking to something live, rather than to old information acquired through a new means.

Thus the Internet moves toward immediacy; and immediacy defines media types, a play on words that suggests an always available media presence. A newspaper is low on the immediacy scale; we read it in the morning knowing that we are seeing a summary of news as it came in several hours before. If an ongoing story catches our eye and we want an update on it, we get the update by flicking on the television, where CNN or one of the major networks points a live camera at the action.

What would stop the growth of the Internet in its tracks would be to forsake that sense of immediacy that the public now demands. Java is one way around the problem; Microsoft's ActiveX technology is another.

Companies like Progressive Networks, with RealAudio, and Xing Technology, with StreamWorks, are pursuing audio and video solutions. This means that if I'm following a major story, I can work at my desk while listening to the news on my computer over the Internet. It was only as the network began to develop these capabilities that the notion of the Net as a challenge to television began to arise. It is emerging as an alternative for viewer time, one that advertisers will have to reckon with as they plan their budgets. Time spent on the Internet is, more and more often, time spent away from the television.

Interacting with Media

If the Web is to compete with television (and, we hope, drive up the intellectual stakes), it must make maximum use of the things that distinguish it from traditional forms of content. On that score, the Web today bears disturbing parallels to CD-ROM technology. Why disturbing? CD-ROMs entered the computer world with immense promise; after all, they could hold more data than a large hard disk, making it possible to digitize entire encyclopedias on a single platter, and to include multimedia features like moving video and sound. But despite prominent exceptions like Microsoft's Encarta (an encyclopedia) and Cinemania (a moviegoer's guide to reviews), CD-ROMs have fallen victim to the "shovelware" phenomenon— it's too easy to put content on them, so developers are careless about the quality of what they sell. Few CD-ROMs on today's market live up to the potential of the medium, as witness the raft of text-based CDs that do nothing other than provide unedited ASCII versions of widely available out-of-copyright texts.

Numerous Web sites have fallen victim to the same carelessness. Out of an imperfect understanding of the medium, their developers have chosen to make the Web little more than a digital form of the printed page. Yes, hyperlinks are included to move you between the various documents at the site, but the potential of multimedia is often lacking, while the notion that people can read vast amounts of text on a computer screen goes unchallenged. To be effective, a Web site must transcend these limitations. The Web is about interactivity, the ability of the user to choose information pathways and explore them with new-found ease. We should be looking for sites that provide something significantly different than the usual reading and researching experience.

How do you translate the experience of television into the World Wide Web format? If you operate The Discovery Channel, the answer is that you provide links to your television shows (including a useful e-mail notification service so your users won't miss shows of particular interest), along with background information supporting your programming. But you also provide original content, using the Web's ability to link to resources that television cannot reach. You make the site an entirely different reason to tune in to the network, and if you're successful, the network benefits from the exposure.

An example of such original content is "Get Down! An Australian Adventure." It appeared on The Discovery Channel's main menu in April 1996, telling the story of one Jim Malusa. In the words of the site: "A man, his bike, and his laptop challenge the merciless outback." Along with the blurb is a photograph of

Malusa that, when clicked, gives way to the underlying page dedicated to his adventures Down Under.

Along one side of that page is a graphical cast of
characters, the people who figure in Malusa's story,
everyone from his mother to the support team who
aided him on his journey. There is a link for someone
called Bikeman, which takes you to John Schubert,
technical editor of *Adventure Cyclist* magazine and
the author of two books on biking. A photograph of
the congenial Schubert likewise appears, along with
two interesting features: At the bottom of the page is a
clickable link that, when chosen, allows you to send
electronic mail to Schubert. An audio link features
Schubert's voice discussing Malusa's proposed journey; he's concerned that the trip will carry the cyclist
into an area so remote that basic supplies will be all
but impossible to obtain.

When you read about a person like John Schubert
in a print magazine, or watch a television show that
covers the Malusa story and see Schubert interviewed,
a rhetorical distance remains between you and the
person discussed. That distance is one reason why it's
so exhilarating for ordinary people when they appear
in the newspaper or on television. The experience is
vivid, almost an out-of-body journey, for what they've
done is to move between one existence, defined by
their daily routine, to another, defined by its presence
on the papers and screens we all use as input devices
for our traditional information.

Electronic mail to the source circumvents that
rhetorical space. Having read what Schubert thinks
about Malusa's proposed trip through Australia, and
having looked at his photograph, we can conflate the
two worlds—the inner and outer experience—by
punching a message straight through to Schubert

himself. The messaging process, enabled by a Web browser, is simple. A click takes us into the editing screen, on which we can compose a message; a second click sends it on its way. With other forms of media, we can, of course, contact the people we see and read about, but the process is more cumbersome, and involves looking up postal addresses, writing letters, or making telephone calls, with no assurance of receiving any response.

Thus hypertext's great potential is interactive. Its linkages can lessen the separation between what we consider news on the one hand and our own experience on the other. Indeed, if we choose, we can bring the newsmaker into our own life by engaging in an electronic mail exchange that allows us to frame questions of our own. How many times have you watched a television show and wondered why a particular question was never asked? Interactive media gives you the chance to ask that question.

The audio link is similarly intriguing. Schubert is an expert on the subject of biking through difficult terrain, so his thoughts on Malusa's trek bear thinking about. When we click on the hyperlink, we begin the download process, pulling in a 400K file which our browser can play by invoking a plug-in audio program. We listen to Schubert's voice as he expresses his thoughts on the various dangers faced by Malusa. The content exists on two levels. We hear the thoughts he's expressing, but we also pick up the nuances of that expression through the spoken word, giving us a feel for his character and personality that we measure against the page's accompanying photograph. The result isn't television—it lacks the immediacy of full-motion video—nor is it straight text. It's a hybrid form of media that works by fleshing out our knowledge step by step, through a series of links that we can explore in whichever direction we choose.

The matter of direction is itself interesting. The top page of the "Get Down!" story contains an image with inset hyperlinks. We can choose between the aforementioned set of people who take part in the story; an introduction to the trip; a map of the journey's progress; updates on Malusa's stopovers, including his letters; and a bulletin board in which people can discuss what's going on as they read through the story and check in to see how Malusa is doing. There is, it's clear, no one way to work through this maze. The picture we build is formed by accretion; we learn in snatches, putting the story together link by link. If a particular aspect of the trip interests us, we can go directly to it, or we can choose to start with the introduction and attempt a chronological perusal of the story.

I chose to begin with an idle click on a person I knew nothing about—John Schubert. I worked into the site knowing that the story must involve a hazardous journey (on a bicycle, of all things) through one of the most inhospitable landscapes on the planet. I listened to Schubert's concerns on an audio clip and then moved on to a current letter from Malusa. Reading it, I discovered he had camped at a place called Nourlangie Rock, near the eastern boundary of Kakadu National Park. I read his thoughts on aboriginal myths and enjoyed his photography.

Maps on the World Wide Web are clickable; at least, they can be. A clickable map is one in which the image overlays deeper content. It's like an atlas that compresses the colorful maps of the first half of the book and the lengthy tables and charts of the second half into a single, dynamic image. Click here to learn more. Click here to return to the larger map. Because I'm obsessed with maps, I want to know where Nourlangie Rock fits into a larger map of Australia, and I find a link to one at the bottom of the page. A click takes me to a map of the entire continent. Here I find that Kakadu National Park is not far outside Darwin, in a part of Australia that is still largely tropical. A click on this map over the dot marking Kakadu takes me to a short backgrounder on this 8,000-square-mile ecosystem, which houses one-third of Australia's bird species and some of its rarest plants and animals.

At each stop along the way, the Web page's designers have made it easy to remember the route. It behooves good Web page designers to always keep a map of the site in front of us, because the Web challenges us with its many different ways to explore its riches. Thus, while our browser can take us back to previous pages with ease, we can also choose to skip directly back to the Introduction screen, or to the Updates page, or to the Bulletin Board on which we can discuss this journey. We can also move between stories at this point, choosing to leave the Malusa adventure and see what other multimedia tales may be stored at the site. A search function provides the ability to enter keywords to return to the page of our choice.

But let's not leave Malusa yet. The Updates page houses the collected letters of the intrepid cyclist as he crosses Australia. This is an ongoing story; it is being updated by its author from the field via laptop computer and Internet connections. I'm looking now at a report of Malusa's encounter with Cyclone Oliver. Having left Kakadu National Park, he noticed increasing clouds; peddling past eucalyptus woodlands, he barely had time to set up his tent and get inside before the storm hit, lashing the canvas with rain and sending stark bolts of lightning across the sky. An accompanying photograph shot by the dispirited Malusa shows the sodden campsite. Storms followed him throughout the rest of his journey through the Northern Territory.

A good Web site, then, is one that continually updates its content. In the case of The Discovery Channel's story on Malusa, I realize that I can check here every day to find out where Jim is on the map and to see the latest photographs of his journey. The material posted seems to be running approximately a day and a half behind actual events, which is presumably the amount of time it takes the developers to translate Jim's letters and photographs into the necessary HTML coding to make up a Web page. It is important here to note how the Web allows me to follow Malusa asynchronously. If I were watching a television account of his exploits, I would need to tune in at the scheduled time. On the Web, I can check at a time of my own choosing.

I also think to click on Jim's own icon, available from the same introductory page to his story. Here I learn that he makes his home in Tucson, Arizona, that he has practiced something called freelance demolition (fireworks?), and that he's a biologist and part-time research associate at the University of Arizona, as well as being a writer, " . . . which seems the correct vocation for someone fond of camping, beans, and travel." The trip through Australia is part of his plan to visit the seven lowest points on each continent. Lake Eyre, his Australian destination, is 50 feet below sea level, a salt lake accessible only through a dirt track leading several hundred miles off the main highway. The accompanying photograph of Jim is of a rugged, self-reliant man who looks tough enough to handle the outback—at least if it's not raining.

At the bottom of the page on Jim's life is a link that looks promising: Click to see all Jim's gear, it says. I do, and am rewarded with a photograph of the lot, spread out on a tarp, each item numbered. Below the photograph is a scrollable field with a key to the numbers. Scrolling through the items, I discover that he is carrying a Kodak digital camera, which is presumably how he's able to get his photographs uploaded and displayed on the Web. His computer is a Toshiba 610 CT, which he's linking to the telephone system through an acoustic coupler that fits onto a conventional telephone handset. That's the only way onto the Internet, long-distance over the rare outback pay phones.

So much for the camera and its digitizing capabilities. But I'm curious about something else. What kind of bicycle does a man take when he's going to journey into one of the most forbidding landscapes on the planet? I decide to take the opportunity to send Malusa a letter of my own, posing this question to him. It's a matter of roughly 24 hours before I receive an answer: "About my bike. After touring with road bikes and mountain bikes, I decided that a hybrid bike is for me. Fast on the road, but I can take it on the dirt, even if it's only a short ways, to get me away from the highway. Mine's a Bruce Gordon Rock 'n Road; very nice, but very expensive if bought new (I found mine used). I've got a set of road wheels and a set of touring wheels, so I simply switch when I get home. Also, I prefer drop handlebars—at least after six or eight hours on the road. But that's a matter of personal preference." By now Malusa is south of Alice Springs, in what, on my map, looks to be totally uninhabited country. And I've been talking to him through my computer.

My wandering through the Malusa story is emblematic of what can happen at a well-planned Web site. I've entered into the story as it was ongoing, prowled around long enough to understand the scenario, returned to read the introductory passages, listened to audio accounts of the planning for the trip, read updates on Malusa's progress, and received additional information on demand. Now I go back to read the letters sequentially, starting out with Jim's departure from the tropical city of Darwin, where " . . . the sun is one mean skillet in the sky," and 4-foot lizards called *goannas* are common sights. An index to the letters makes it easy to skip around between them, but I'm now reading sequentially, following from link to link, in chronological order. I'm filling in my background information and catching up on what I've missed.

One hyperlink is as close as another on the World Wide Web. Thus far, I've stayed within The Discovery Channel's Web site, but one link takes me to a page that displays links to other Web sources. I find Australia Online, with Australian maps, news, and tourist information. The Aboriginal Page, from Australian National University, contains extensive information about aboriginal culture. Diction-Aussie is an interactive Australian dictionary, which can explain cryptic sentences like this one uttered to Jim in Darwin by a man with felt hat and tattoos: "I was once working a mob of brumbies on a station when a jackeroo asked the boss cockie what to do if he runs across a western taipan." It translates: "I was once rounding up a herd of wild horses when a cowboy asked the foreman how to avoid a venomous snake."

There is no up or down at a Web site. While the introductory page to the Malusa story could legitimately be considered a gateway into it, most readers will come into the tale by clicking here and there, sampling from among the many sights and sounds of the associated documents, to form their own experience of the story. The experience can be extended by sending electronic mail to people involved in the journey or by joining the bulletin board likewise made available to readers. A Web site without such interactivity is one that fails to deliver on the promise of the medium.

Interactivity is one of the three key concepts that help the Web deliver on that promise. All three start with the letter *I*: interactivity, immediacy, and integration. *Interactivity*, because a well-designed site lets you talk to the players and conceivably influence the way a particular situation is handled; interactivity also means being able to choose your own path through the site. *Immediacy*, because a frequently updated Web site can put you on the scene of a continuing story, just as I check in every day to track the progress of a cyclist through the Australian outback. And finally, *integration*, because a good Web site exploits varied forms of media to support its message. Learning how to turn this hybrid medium to your advantage means mastering a set of tools designed expressly for the purpose of cataloging and retrieving Web resources.

CHAPTER

Searching the
Virtual Library

*The maddening thing about the virtual library is that
it's not a digitization of the real library at all,
although the instances of overlap are growing. Rather,
it's a second, parallel library that's growing according
to its own rules.*

Wake County, North Carolina, where I live and work,
has made life difficult for the independent researcher.
Although it's hard to fathom in an area surrounded by
Duke University, UNC-Chapel Hill, and North Carolina State, Raleigh has largely given up on the public
library. Living here, I've learned that circulation
numbers, not quality, are used to determine which
books to put on the library shelf. Older volumes are
sold off in a merciless triage operation every year, to
finance the purchase of multiple copies of the latest
best-sellers for each of the Wake County branch
libraries. Needless to say, reference services dwindle
while romance novels and celebrity biographies proliferate.

In this environment, I turned to computer networking to find the kind of archival tools I needed. In

essence, archives are the reason I began experimenting with the Internet and commercial on-line services. Historically, on-line research has proceeded through commercial content providers, which made large databases of information available for a fee. These companies, like DIALOG and Dow Jones News/Retrieval, proceeded to sell services under a pay-by-the-minute model, coupled with a monthly or yearly subscription charge. I could, for example, sign up for a DIALOG account that let me search hundreds of publications, from general-interest newsstand magazines to obscure journals aimed at specialists, at a rate that varied by the database.

Every time I ran a search, though, I first had to determine which database I needed by cross-referencing the extensive documentation DIALOG provided (and I do mean extensive—four huge three-ring-binder notebooks!). I would then log on, give the command to call up a particular database, and enter the criteria for the information I needed. It was expensive, but in the absence of a passable library, it was all I had.

It is this subscription-based model of information that the Internet explicitly challenges. Just as traditional news publications are experimenting with on-line services, hoping to determine whether there are ways to provide content by computer while retaining their traditional reader base, so content providers of all stripes are wrestling with the issue of archives. The archival dilemma is this: Free content cuts the ground from underneath the commercial database providers and calls into question a given publication's financial viability. Widely distributing copyrighted materials raises major issues about on-line payment mechanisms to ensure that author and publisher are compensated for their intellectual efforts. But Internet users, especially researchers, are demanding wider access to back issues and related reference materials. Their growing numbers constitute a market the content providers can scarcely afford to ignore.

Publishers are behind the curve on this issue because they're still locked into the subscription format. But forcing readers to subscribe to a year's worth of a particular publication or service is a concept that has outrun its usefulness. Consider the print world alone, where thousands of magazines and scholarly journals vie for your attention; who can possibly subscribe to them all? Even those few to which we do subscribe tend to pile up unread, quickly become obsolete, and end up curbside, material for the recycler. With computer publications, following a single magazine inevitably means you miss news and features that might have caught your eye in another—a frustrating experience for anyone determined to stay abreast of this rapidly changing environment.

In the world of on-line research, this subscription model inherently limits the range of information available. DIALOG, Nexis, and Dow Jones News/Retrieval are all database services that require you to log on with a password and pay by-the-minute charges to access their databases. Their holdings are far-reaching; Nexis, for example, contains the full text of *The New York Times*, while Dow Jones News/Retrieval provides the same service for *The Wall Street Journal*, not to mention hundreds of other journals, newspapers, newsletters, and financial databases. Services like NewsNet focus on specialized datasets; NewsNet's holdings are limited to low-circulation newsletters, while Burrelle's Broadcast Database provides transcripts of broadcast news and talk shows.

These services, though, extensive as they are, profoundly circumscribe what the average researcher can do. To run a thorough search on, say, the soft drink market in Argentina, you would be able to use any of the big three database services—DIALOG, Nexis, or Dow Jones. But inevitably, a search through one service would turn up references to articles not available within its database. Perhaps DIALOG would provide you with an abstract of a potentially valuable article that was found in full-text form only on Nexis. Thus a complete search (at least, as complete as is possible given the current state of the art) would involve subscribing to *all* the database services, which is prohibitively expensive unless you run a research-oriented business.

The last search I ran on DIALOG cost over $100 to generate 89 references—just bibliographical information, mind you, not full-text—to articles that dealt in some way with my topic. In this environment, the clock emphatically ticks; every moment you spend on-line has a dollar sign attached. Once you formulate a search query, you go on-line only long enough to execute it and capture the results in a disk file, to be examined after you have logged off. And determining the search criteria itself is a complex process of defining keywords and phrases that employ so-called Boolean logic, a way of stating a query that uses connectors such as AND or NOT in a highly formalized way. Clearly, this is a job for specialists—which is how the information-brokerage business makes its money.

The commercial database grew up in a world where computer resources were expensive and rare. It was not designed for an environment in which the average business and home contain a computer. Remarkably, the necessity for appealing to a broader audience has seemingly not occurred to the more established players in this game, who remain content to mine corporate sources for their revenues. But the coming wave of content creation on the Internet is open, democratic, and user-friendly. In a sharp departure from the subscription model, its costs are minimal and its developing microtransaction technology will soon provide ways to reimburse content providers and authors with royalties, making the addition of copyrighted material to the existing Internet archives a certainty. This becomes apparent when we consider the library, and how library science has learned to catalog its holdings.

Of Catalogs and Carrier Pigeons

Cataloging and indexing is what people with large information resources do. The commercial computer databases represented the first great wave of digital research in this area. Created to manage massive amounts of raw data (DIALOG, for example, grew out of Lockheed's work with NASA and the rapidly accumulating desiderata of the race for the moon), they offered researchers the chance to perform retrieval wonders never before possible for the individual. To run a single keyword or search phrase through a stack of 70,000 documents and return all documents containing that keyword is potent magic to a world accustomed to scanning paper indices and tables of contents one by one, or consulting bound volumes of bibliographic data page by painstaking page.

The card catalog has always been the critical library index. After all, libraries are huge collections;

some estimates of the holdings at the ancient Library of Alexandria go as high as 700,000 scrolls, while today's Library of Congress in Washington is a fully multimedia collection housing not only millions of individual volumes, but also maps, recordings, digital information, microfilms, microfiche, and other forms of media; its collection currently covers material written in some 470 different languages. The catalog system created by Melvil Dewey in 1876 and revised 19 times since then has made cataloging and retrieving books in such holdings practical, although in recent times the Library of Congress itself has created a more refined classification method suitable for larger collections. In either case, however, the concept of cataloging depends upon knowledge classification, and the application of exceedingly fine-grained judgments about subject matter and placement within the collection.

The Dewey system, for example, divided all knowledge into 10 categories, each of which was designated by a numerical spread between 1 and 1,000. Reference works like encyclopedias and dictionaries occupied the first slot, with numbers from 000 to 099, while the range from 700 to 799 included the arts and related subjects, and so on. Subclasses within these ranges then divided each into appropriate categories, with indexing proceeding down to decimal points after individual numbers. The latter indicate information such as the period of a particular work's appearance or its subject matter.

The Library of Congress classification similarly divides knowledge, only this time into 21 categories, each of which can be indicated by a capital letter: H stands for works on the social sciences, T for technology, D for universal history, and so on. Subcategories are then indicated by combinations of capital letters, while three-digit identifiers can be further used to specify unique topics. In each case, the principle is to apply human judgment to divide knowledge into sub-groupings, so that broader subjects can be broken continually into narrower ones, until we arrive at the level of the individual book. Needless to say, a large part of the skill of library science is in the ability to make the necessary judgments about where new additions to a collection are to be placed.

Can the Internet perform a similar function? If I were to create an analogy between the Internet and a library, as so many writers on this topic have done, I would have to acknowledge that the network is in some ways in the dark ages of information retrieval. Whereas the broadly accepted cataloging work of Dewey didn't come into acceptance until late in the nineteenth century, it was nonetheless true that individual libraries cataloged their works according to principles of their own; information retrieval was possible, if cumbersome, at Alexandria or, for that matter, the 20,000-scroll library created in 1250 B.C. by the Egyptian pharaoh Ramses II. Books may have been scarce in the medieval scriptoria, but monks knew how to find them.

Not so with the Internet; at least, not until recently. For one thing, content has always been questionable on the network, for in the early days ARPANET was used as a research network, of value solely to the specialists who transferred their ideas and datasets across it. The notion that it would grow into a repository of broadly based information had not yet emerged. When the universities began to maximize the potential of networking in the 1980s, and libraries first started putting their library catalogs on-line, data storage was decidedly parochial in nature. A given system administrator would create an archive of mailing list postings on a specific computer; that archive could be searched using the text-based protocols demanded by the mailing list software, but doing so required relatively sophisticated knowledge and procedures which were anything but user-friendly. The ANSAX-L mailing list, for example, was created as a communications channel for medieval scholars, whose postings were then saved in the list archive. To get at older material, you had to submit keywords with a precise set of commands to the computer running the operation. Make one typing mistake and the search would fail.

Meanwhile, information moving onto the network grew exponentially, supplemented by tools designed to make retrieval easier. Gopher grew up as a menu-based system for academics and students at the University of Minnesota. By moving an on-screen pointer to a particular menu item, the user could quickly summon that item to the screen without having to enter a complex UNIX command. The name Gopher implies a creature that burrows through a space to dig out information, but a better analogy might be to a carrier pigeon that brings a specific message directly to you. Although replacing a naked command prompt with a more intuitive interface broadened the ability of faculty and administrators to do productive work on the Internet, it also meant that content providers had to provide materials on-line that made it worthwhile to use the technology.

Various search tools grew out of the realization that finding things on the Internet was the researcher's greatest problem. Veronica, for example, was a tool that allowed you to search Gopher menus for specific keywords; it would return its findings as links to the Gopher menus in question, so that you could quickly check the contents of a file no matter what its location. Unfortunately, Veronica was limited in its functionality and was bypassed as Gopher itself gave way to the World Wide Web.

The advent of the Web was, in fact, the defining moment for Internet-based research. Designed to allow specialists to share information, the Web proved that you could readily link data that people already knew about; unfortunately, you couldn't easily show them where to find that data in the first place. It was one thing to create a Web site in common use by a community of physicists, but what happened when you wanted to offer an archive of recipes, a collection of essays, or a gallery of photographs to the world at large? How could the world beat a path to your door when the path was uncharted, uncataloged, and could be discovered only serendipitously?

Starting the Search Engine

The search engine is the answer to many of the dilemmas posed by the World Wide Web. Extending the definition of the term *engine*, it refers to the software tools that power the search process. Sporting names like Excite, Inktomi, AltaVista, WebCrawler, and Lycos, these search tools have become some of the hottest products of the Internet era—and for good reason. Now proliferating in the hundreds, they offer users the ability to search widely for terms that appear on individual home pages. And they produce their lists of results in hypertextual form; you just click on one of them to visit the page in question. If spreadsheets were the application that made personal computers take off in small businesses and homes, search engines are performing a similar feat for the Internet. The key question is, how do these search engines fit into our conception of the Internet as a kind of library?

The ultimate goal of network visionaries is the construction of an on-line reference work that contains the sum of all human knowledge from the days of the first cave paintings to the latest scientific breakthroughs—what Michael Hart, the founder of Project Gutenberg, likes to call an Encyclopedia Galactica. If the Internet is to achieve that goal, it will take all the skills of present-day library science and all the power of tomorrow's technology with regard to speed and bandwidth to make it happen.

Using these search engines is significantly different from working your way through a traditional card catalog—for a variety of reasons. The search begins simply enough: You tell your Web browser to access a specific site. Digital Equipment's AltaVista engine, for example, uses the following URL: http://www.altavista. digital.com/. It's a typical address, as are those of all the major search engines; you are logging on to a remote computer to access a home page, just as you would at any other Web site. But in this case, rather than being presented with a simple screen full of graphics or text, you're shown a keyword field. The idea is to choose a word or phrase that describes what you're looking for and enter it. You then click a button or press a Return to begin the search. Your keyword(s) are run through a huge database maintained and regularly updated at the search engine site, and soon the list of results is displayed, usually in multiple pages of hypertextual information.

Search engines differ in how they create their databases, but the general principle is to send a so-called software robot out onto the Internet to follow links from one Web page to another, cataloging the content at each. These tools, sometimes called *spiders*, are constantly on the prowl to uncover new hyperlinks—no mean job in a medium as malleable as today's Web. If you broke a search engine into its constituent parts, then, you would find the following: the underlying search retrieval mechanism (a Web robot or spider); the database in which the robot puts its results, and against which search queries are run; and the search interface, which is what you see on-screen when you use the site.

The spider metaphor explains the names of some of these engines. Lycos, for example, created at Carnegie Mellon University, is named for a member of the arachnid family that aggressively hunts down its prey, while another popular engine, Inktomi, is named after a mythological spider prominent in Plains Indian culture. Other engines use more generic names, such as InfoSeek, a combination of free and fee-based information, or Yahoo!, a famous engine that grew originally out of a simple directory of Internet sites and has become one of the most frequented pages on the Internet. A recent trend has been to combine searches by offering single-keyword sweeps through multiple sites.

But whatever the name and methodology, the idea is to provide a form of indexing and quick retrieval for widely dispersed content. The search engine is the Internet's answer to the Dewey decimal and the

Library of Congress cataloging schemes. While some old hands on the Internet fear that such cataloging will lead to a loss of spontaneity and innovation, the path forward seems clear: Without reliable cataloging services, the Internet's growth into a reliable research tool would be aborted.

The Words Are Key

Older database systems generally did their work using the aforementioned Boolean search terms, keywords connected by specific words to form logical statements. Named after George Boole, a nineteenth-century British mathematician who studied the relationship between mathematics and logic, these so-called Boolean operators had to be carefully placed so that the search would proceed accurately. The statement *science fiction and heinlein*, for example, would search the full text of all documents in the database, looking for those that contained both the terms *science fiction* and *heinlein*. The statement *science fiction not heinlein* would seek out all documents containing the term *science fiction* but specifically excluding the term *heinlein*. Using connectors like AND, NOT, OR, and others, it was possible to create a highly sophisticated search strategy. Some Internet search engines continue to use Boolean statements as one way in which keywords can be connected.

But other keyword strategies have become available, methods more suited to the average user. Natural-language queries, for instance, are those that resemble ordinary speech, the kind of question you might ask in conversation. And many engines let you simply enter the major parts of your search concept without worrying about syntax. If I were looking for information about Robert Heinlein's novel *The Door into Summer*, for example, I might simply list as my search phrase the following statement: *science fiction heinlein summer*. The search engine would then look for all these terms, returning hits matching some or all of them. Some of the hits, presumably those at the top of the list, would include all four search words. Others might include just two or even one. This is why it's possible to run such a search and wind up with a Web page talking about summer in the Catskills as one of your responses. The word *summer*, after all, was listed among the keywords to be searched.

Obviously, determining the appropriate keywords is, well, key. The HotBot engine, for example, assumes that the AND operator is inserted between multiple keywords; as opposed to the preceding search, it would generate a list only of those sites that use every one of the words. The AltaVista engine, whose URL is listed in the previous example, makes a contrary assumption; it assumes an OR connector, producing pages that contain any of the relevant terms. To tell AltaVista to produce a list of hits containing each of my words, I would need to connect the words with an AND (I could also, at many search sites, use a plus (+) symbol to achieve the same result).

How do you know which engine makes what assumptions? The only solution is to work your way with care through each engine's home page, looking for descriptive information about how it works. Many engines, for example, let you put quotation marks around phrases as a way of limiting your results only to Web pages that contain the phrase exactly as written. This useful strategy is a quick solution to many search problems, but only if you know to use it. Another useful strategy is to exclude words, which some search engines allow you to do with a minus (-) sign. If you're getting too many hits for a workable result, you can exclude broad categories of documents by determining what the pages you *don't* want to see have in common and excluding it.

The best approach with most search engines is to keep the search as straightforward as possible. My procedure is to make a list of words and phrases that should appear in any document I want to see, comprising the major concepts or statements that define my material. A search for Web pages specializing in on-line education, for example, might include words like *syllabus*, *class*, *faculty*, *lecture*, and, of course, *education*. Critical to a good search is to use multiple keywords. Entering three or four search terms is invariably more precise than using a single one, as the dizzying growth of the Web all but ensures that you'll receive hundreds, if not thousands, of mostly irrelevant hits when you search loosely. A tight search strategy, combining keywords and requiring that they appear in the same document, will keep your list of results manageable.

The degree of precision you decide to bring to the search process is up to you, but it behooves you to understand how search engines differ. Every time you enter a keyword or phrase, you are setting up a filter against which the search engine will run its entire database. The world of search engines has become competitive and commercialized, as witness engines like Yahoo! and Lycos, which are now publicly traded companies. Any edge that developers can give a specific engine will be exploited, which means we'll continue to see new search methods. The best procedure to master them is to print out available tips, lists of operators, delimiters, and techniques, and save them, particularly if you plan to make frequent use of a particular engine. Always explore an engine's home page to locate such materials before running a search.

Sifting Out the Ore

Web-based search engines introduce numerous issues in terms of how we find and evaluate information. In common with other Internet technologies, these software tools have a disquieting tendency to make decisions for us—or, to put it perhaps more accurately, we have a tendency to let them do so. The problem with retrieving search results of any kind, whether from a commercial database like DIALOG or a World Wide Web search engine, is evaluating what we've found. And this proves to be an exceedingly difficult issue, given the flexible nature of the Web-based search and the fact that most search engines retrieve based on our search parameters. This problem becomes clear when you consider, first, the likely size of the dataset we can generate with a given search. The AltaVista database, for example, was processing several million queries daily just months after its appearance on the Internet, drawing on a list of 10 billion keywords taken from over 30 million Web sites in sweeps by its search robots. Every improvement to the search routines it uses and every increase in the number and variety of Web servers causes those figures to increase.

Next consider that a particular search engine displays its hits according to how its programmers have constructed the interface. In general, a small number of results will be displayed, with the option to show as many more as you might like to see. Thus I might run the previous search (*science fiction heinlein summer*) and come up with 10 hits, each of which contains all or most of my search terms. I can page through the list and choose to visit any of the Web pages shown on it. But at the bottom of the list I find that there is a link to another 10 hits, a display of further results. And following that page of 10, another page of 10, and so on. I've run searches that pulled in thousands of hits, although many engines set an upper limit; in other words, additional pages meeting my criteria may have been out there, but the search engine, working within the limits of its own programming, has been programmed to display only a particular number.

To bypass this limitation, search engines generally attempt to present their results using a process called *relevancy ranking*, which refers to the way they evaluate the documents they find. A search engine can provide a particular weighting to the occurrences of your search terms in each document. Using a variety of methods, such as counting which documents contain the most search terms and which use a particular term with the greatest frequency, the software presents its results according to what it *assumes* you want. Theoretically, the items at the top of your list ought to be the best, while those at the bottom are correspondingly less valuable; the further you work your way into the set of results, the less useful each returned item becomes. The operative word here is *theoretically*. In fact, the typical search screen can be profoundly misleading.

Why? Technology has always created a plausibility problem in the minds of its users; simply put, people believe what they see if it's presented with enough technological panache, which is why there are people who accept everything they watch on television or read in the newspapers. That problem is exacerbated by computers, for in the case of search engines, we're dealing with what appears to be a highly mediated and effective search process run by machines with search skills far greater than our own. We human beings can't sift through millions of pages of text in the space of a few seconds, so we attach credibility to the technology that can.

The result? Many of us are tempted to run an Internet search, look at the first screen of results, and assume we've seen the best the Internet has to offer on our topic. The assumption fails on two counts. First, the search engine's relevancy ranking is based on arbitrary criteria, which often fail to anticipate our actual needs; in any case, we may not have stated our search terms with the greatest of clarity, or we may have forgotten a key term that could have changed the nature of the search. Second, because each search engine works with its own database, created by its own software tools, if we run the same search on a different engine the results could be markedly different.

Does this mean you can't trust search engines? Of course not. But it places a premium upon your own ingenuity. Just as the Internet demands critical reading—editorial decision making—of its users, so it demands research skills of an uncommon sort from those who would mine it as an information resource. The Internet researcher has to be more persistent, more doggedly devoted to rooting out the data, than his or her book bound counterpart. When a search is important, you'll find yourself going through the results screen after screen. The item you need may be the 129th hit listed by the search engine, and you won't find that out unless you work entirely through the list.

Tedious? Of course. But now we're back to the admonition that search terms shouldn't be so broad as to generate hundreds of hits in the first place. If the number of results becomes truly unmanageable, the best thing to do is revise your search strategy so that it will produce fewer hits. This may involve choosing search terms that must appear adjacent to each other, or within close proximity; most search engines allow you to specify such couplings. It may mean searching for a particular phrase but excluding a term that is likely to produce misleading hits. Depending upon the search engine, it might involve using the minus sign as mentioned, capitalizing proper names, putting brackets around keywords, or using quotation marks to specify whole phrases.

The best advice is to locate a search engine that suits your needs and focus on it alone. There will be ample time to learn about the other engines once you've mastered the basic tenets of searching. Initially, just pick one of the major sites—Lycos, Yahoo!, AltaVista, HotBot, InfoSeek—and get to know it from the top down. Master every nuance of its methodology by reading the file of tips and techniques it provides. Spending time with this material now will pay off as you begin to broaden your searching to other sites and learn how to apply the same principles to search engines with a different structure.

The Search Engine as Card Catalog

Recall that I posed the question as to how search engines fit the conception of the Internet as library. In short, search engines are the components of the Internet's catalog. But their lack of standardization reminds us that it is early to be drawing such a comparison. Consider the outcome if every public library in the world used its own cataloging scheme to shelve its books. Each time you entered a different library, you would have to study its cataloging system in order to determine how to find a particular book or magazine. This is where we are on the Internet today. Each search engine, streamlining itself to face an increasingly commercialized environment, requires a similar effort to master its idiosyncrasies.

As a result of its multimedia format, the Internet library raises difficult archival issues for the next generation of cyberlibrarian. What do we do, for example, with a growing archive of letters from the field, of the kind we saw Jim Malusa sending from Australia to The Discovery Channel's Web site? Each of the letters is linked to audio and video resources, and in some cases to other Web sites with related information. The archive includes clickable maps, commentary from specialists, and links to discussion groups keyed to reader participation. It must be cataloged in some comprehensive way—but how? How would such a collection appear in standard Dewey decimal terms?

A card catalog works something like a form-driven database. When you create such a database, you first ponder what kind of template to use. Assume I want to create a database of business contacts. I might start by taking out a yellow notepad and jotting down which categories were most valuable to me. First would be the person's name, and second would be the name of his or her company. I would want a field for the person's telephone number, a second for the fax number, and surely a third for an e-mail address. I would want a fairly flexible field in which to put notes from each telephone call, and I might also like some way to link to previous telephone calls with this person. Making decisions like these lets me create a personalized information space, which I can then arrange according to the categories, or fields, I have created.

Only at this point would I actually turn to my database software and begin to create the template that would hold these fields. When I had done so, each time I called up a blank record, the fields would be opened for me to fill in. A conventional card catalog functions precisely this way, in the sense that the categories have been chosen by trained librarians who understand the need for accuracy in tracking archival material. The categories, in other words, are standardized; each library functions essentially like any other. If I want to search for books by H. Rider Haggard, I can use the author's name to run my search, or I can use the title of one of his books, such as *King Solomon's Mines*.

Now notice what I can't do with the standard card catalog template. In the days before computers, certain types of retrieval could only be managed by human memory. Consider what would happen if I were trying to find a particular quotation, like this one:

> "As the long line of the mountain coast unfolded before me
> I had an optical illusion; it may be that many have had it
> before. As new lengths of coast and lines of height were
> unfolded, I had the fancy that the whole land was not
> receding but advancing, like something spreading out its
> arms to the world. A chance shred of sunshine rested, like
> a riven banner, on the hill which I believe is called in Irish
> the Mountain of the Golden Spears; and I could have
> imagined that the spear and the banner were coming on.
> And in that flash I remembered that the men of this
> island had once gone forth, not with the torches of con-
> querors or destroyers, but as missionaries in the very
> midnight of the Dark Ages; like a multitude of moving
> candles, that were the light of the world."

Suppose I go to a physical library with this quotation and *nothing else*. I tell the librarian that I don't know who wrote it, and I'm not sure what it's about, nor do I have the title of a book that might contain it. In the absence of something to put in the card catalog's information fields, what can the librarian do? Perhaps the best bet would be to examine the subject matter, which clearly relates to Ireland and its history after the fall of Rome, and look for books that treat that history. But as you can see, that would be a lengthy and a cumbersome process, and it's not one that's likely to produce a result.

By contrast, the virtual library with its search engines is not stymied by this quotation, for the search engine allows me to look for things other than field-driven information. The difference between the real and the virtual library in terms of cataloging is the difference between a form-driven database and a free-form database. The latter is one that puts no constraints on how data is entered. And when we search it, we can search anywhere in the full text of a document to find what we need. In the absence of an author or a title, we can run a search on a phrase, such as the lovely "Mountain of the Golden Spears" line that occurs in the quoted passage. If that phrase is located somewhere in the search engine's database, the software will find it. And we would learn that the quotation is from a 1919 title by G. K. Chesterton called *Irish Impressions*.

Full-text versus field-defined. The distinction is powerful and productive. With full-text search capabilities, not only do we put the power of the microprocessor to work to search by brute computer force through massive amounts of information, but we also conduct a fundamentally different kind of search, one that librarians of the past would not have been capable of attempting. The implications for information retrieval are immense; suddenly, the "information at your fingertips" cliché that appears in so many casual discussions about the Internet seems to take on life. The virtual library, the one without walls or card catalogs, lets us take a single thought, concept, or quotation and run it through millions of networked pages of hypertext as a query. From the standpoint of retrieval alone, the virtual library has the potential to be a significant step forward for library science.

Notice that I said potential; this is the crucial caveat, because all this is possible only if the *content* to support such retrieval is made available on-line. In today's world, we face the dilemma that most of the world's information has yet to be digitized. Yes, we can examine extensive databases of material created within the past five years, and in some cases can go back into the 1980s to locate articles that correspond to our data needs. But information in digital format before 1980 or so is remarkably sparse. If, say, I were to try to call up an issue of the *Proceedings of the Modern Language Association* from 1965, I would be out of luck. I can't read *Time*'s coverage of the Normandy invasion on-line, nor can I see what *The New York Times* said about the death of Gandhi. Digital information, in other words, is generally recent in provenance and limited in subject. We're only at the beginning of the digital revolution that will transform older analog information into the bits and bytes that computers can hyperlink around the globe.

The Engine and the Matrix

In a powerful speech delivered at the EDMedia conference in 1995, Laura Fillmore, president of Open Books Systems, called on-line publishing ". . . a potent complement to—and not a substitute for—our existing print culture."[1] Pointing to what she calls "hyperliteracy," a form of knowledge gathering made possible by HTML, she said, "The key challenge for the hypertext literate consists in how the author's text is accessed, by whom, and to what end, and also how the meaning of an author's text changes color when it is contextualized through juxtapositional linking."[2] This is another way of saying that on-line works, as opposed to their physical cousins like books and newspapers, draw added meaning from the universe of documents and other media surrounding them.

A conventional library, of course, does the same thing for each book within it; the individual book is shaped by the collective context of the library's holdings. But hypertext brings us the opportunity to make that context tangible; the individual hyperlink connects us to other views with far greater speed than a reference in a printed volume. It is essential to think about the research experience in much the same way—it is an individually determined exploration of related ideas. A good hypertext author makes it happen by creating links: Click here to read the State Department's official response to the taking of an American hostage. Click here to read off-the-record remarks by a high administration official, who speaks only on condition that his or her name not be used. Click here to read the hostage-taker's demands. All provide context and depth to our research. And all can be supplemented by less official sources; we can link to discussion areas set up for people to talk about the issues, or to Web sites that provide useful background.

Fillmore refers to the growing body of on-line work as a "kinetic and customizable palimpsest."[3] A palimpsest is an early manuscript from which the writing was once removed so that the scribe could reuse the papyrus or parchment it was written on. The early Middle Ages were a time when writing materials were scarce, particularly after the supply of papyrus from Egypt was cut off during the Crusades. When a papyrus was washed to remove its text, or a parchment was erased, fragments from the earlier work were often left behind, still visible to later scholars. Thus we have parts of Homer's *Iliad* preserved in the document called the Codex Nitriensis, which also contains snatches of Euclid, the material still recognizable despite the intended use of the manuscript for a much later religious treatise.

A palimpsest represents the chance survival of ancient materials, whereas the universe of hypertextual information allows the virtually infinite replication of related works of information. But the notion that one work can somehow "contain" another is at the core of the hypertext experience. In an environment where the presentation of argument and background is equally shared with the need to link properly to diverse views, the Internet's holdings themselves are seen as a flexible and continuously expanding record of humanity. As Fillmore notes, this Great Record was first suggested by Vannevar Bush in 1945.[4] And as Bush's work seems to imply, an open Internet means that placing work in context becomes essential. Indeed, if an author fails to do so, someone else will do it for him, through appropriate links off other pages to the author's work.

We have not yet entered the era of the Great Record. Witnesses to the laying of its foundations, we are creating an information cache drawing on the Net's ability to collect media and to preserve the datapaths that we take through it. An electronic book becomes enriched with the collected contributions of readers, whose own thoughts on the issue at hand, left as postings on a linked newsgroup, can themselves become pointers to information. Recognizing the elastic nature of the Web's holdings, we can see that the search engine is the only cataloging tool that could work here; only its constant updating and relentless Web scouring can keep pace with the growing matrix that surrounds each idea site. The very connectedness of Net information also creates publishing issues when we try to relate what will appear on-line with the traditional world of print. As we'll see, one model now being explored to support Net-based publishing is to make the text of a copyrighted book freely available, while charging for access to supporting discussions, chat areas, and hyperlinks.

Such issues are a world away from the work of Melvil Dewey, a fact that further drives home the distinction between the virtual and physical libraries.

Taking the Library On-Line

Given that distinction, it's puzzling that the convergence between the virtual library and the real one has taken on so traditional an aspect. Yes, it's true that hundreds of libraries are now on the Internet, but in this context, being "on the Internet" means that the library in question has made its *card catalog*—not the contents of that card catalog—available on-line. On a rainy evening, I can use my modem to access this catalog instead of driving out to the physical building to look at the shelves. I can find out whether the book I need is available or checked out, a convenience, to be sure, but hardly a breakthrough in the technology of data retrieval.

I call up the library catalog and find a copy of Plutarch's *Moralia*, a 16-volume set of essays and observations made available by the Loeb Classical Library. Because I anticipate weekend guests, I need volume 3. It contains the famous essay "The Dinner of the Seven Wise Men," which provides the immortal guidance that the number of guests at a dinner party should number no more than nine (the number of the Muses) and no fewer than three (the number of the Graces). There is the book in digitally cataloged form on my screen. I can see the full entry, but now what? What do I do to read the text? The answer is, I go to the "real" library and take it off the shelf.

Thus, the maddening thing about the virtual library is that it's not a digitization of the real library at all, although the instances of overlap are growing. Rather, it's a second, parallel library that's growing according to its own rules. The virtual library is made up of the individual contributions of researchers, editors, publishers, television and radio stations, newspapers, and all those who have laid some claim on this digital frontier. In some cases, the work they have created contains inset content from their more traditional publications, and hence converges with the physical library at least as far as text is concerned. But in most cases, the hypertext pages we read, with their linked graphics, sound, and e-mail, are a form of content available only on-line. The separation between virtual and real library is a gulf that divides one form of publishing from another.

A variety of projects have sprung up to aid the virtual library in acquiring at least some of the real library's resources. Project Gutenberg, run out of Illinois Benedictine College, is a volunteer effort to digitize classic works of European literature and spread them widely on the Internet. The Online Book Initiative is another such project. In both cases, material that has moved into the public domain (its copyright has expired) is digitized either through the use of a scanner or by the painstaking typing of volunteers. The Internet becomes the distribution medium for those who want to access these books.

But here again we come up against the limitations of the present virtual library. Volunteer efforts take a long time to produce results, while issues regarding textual variations and version control remain—which Shakespeare do you use, as edited by whom? In any case, a look through the current holdings of both these projects shows that they contain a small subset of the real library's materials, and in almost every case maintain a single edition of each work rather than multiple versions produced by different editors. It's as if, having converted all phonographs to CD players, we found ourselves with only a single playable version of each Beethoven symphony.

Given this division, what is our goal? The principle behind the virtual library must be to support and significantly expand the capabilities of the real library. Rather than supplanting books and magazines, the virtual library on the Internet must become a place where content is equally available, albeit in different form. I would like to be able to check a book out of the real library or find the same book on the network. The two books, identical in terms of the words that make them up, are vastly different in terms of the access they offer. One is for long-haul reading: The physical book is what I bring to the easy chair in front of my fireplace to read, to explore, to mull over with a glass of wine. The virtual book is the one I call up on-screen when I need information. Unlike the physical book, the virtual book can be manipulated, searched, rearranged, dissected. I can ask the virtual Plutarch for every instance of the word honor and thereby learn something about classical notions of humanity. Or I can read the physical Plutarch, absorbing the same material at leisure, reading for the pleasure of the experience and the enjoyment of the narrative. This is a fundamentally different reading experience, less research-oriented, more holistic in approach. The first method, via the virtual book, is inductive, scientific; the second, via the physical book, is deductive and humane.

A Match Made in Cyberspace: Computers and Copyright

We need both kinds of libraries. But clearly, significant issues must be resolved before the physical and virtual libraries coexist in this fashion. The primary stumbling block is the nature of copyright law and the assumptions that underpin it. If a publishing company makes money by selling tangible objects called books, how can it be convinced to put those same books on-line, given that they could then be accessed, mined for their information, and readily copied? Wouldn't such books quickly lose their clout in the marketplace, so that sales in the bookstores dwindled? What would prevent people from reading books on-line and never buying the printed version? And doesn't the same reservation hold true about on-line magazines and newspapers?

These are reasonable concerns, and the answers to them are diverse, for there are several possible models to support the merger between the two libraries. To explain them, we need to understand what copyright is for. If I write a book, I, or those I have licensed, have the exclusive right to reproduce it. No one else will be able to take the words I have written and make use of them without my permission (with obvious concessions to reviewers who need to quote particular parts of the book in their work, and so on; this is what is meant by the term *fair use*). U.S. copyright law makes a productive distinction between the expression of ideas and the ideas themselves; my ideas can be restated in different ways without infringing on my copyright, whereas my exact expression of those ideas is protected. The distinction is productive because it allows ideas to be restated and clarified, a worthwhile part of any intellectual enterprise. Copyright protection is itself productive, because it encourages the creator of intellectual property to put ideas to work in the expectation of making money.

U.S. copyright law has been changed numerous times since its introduction in 1790; in recent times, the Copyright Act of 1976 decreed that copyright takes effect automatically as soon as a work is created and lasts for the duration of the author's life plus 50 years. This extension of copyright means that unpublished works, and works that have been published but not registered with the copyright office of the Library of Congress, are granted the same legal protection as works that have been registered. Registration nonetheless has its benefits, for cash penalties for copyright infringement remain higher for registered materials. The recent General Agreement on Trade and Tariffs (GATT) caused U.S. law to change, extending the period of copyright protection from life plus 50 to life plus 70 years.

With various provisions for the sale or licensing of copyright, the production of copies in libraries, and the extension of copyright to types of media beyond the textual, copyright law moves into the international realm through the Universal Copyright Convention, which extends the same copyright protection to foreign works as it does to domestic. Some 70 countries support the UCC because of the common belief in protecting an author's work from unauthorized distribution, which, in turn, protects the publishers who contract with the author to produce that work in print. A publisher loses if the book it has paid to produce is hijacked by someone else and made available at a lower price, just as the author loses out on potential royalty payments.[5]

Given this system of protection, codified, ratified, and subject to hundreds of years of scrutiny (the first copyright law in Britain goes back to the Statute of Anne in 1709), it's clear that the Internet's virtual library poses a serious challenge.[6] Unlike a real book, a virtual book can be copied in its entirety in seconds; it can be duplicated numerous times, sent around the world as e-mail, printed out on local printers, and read off-line. If that book is to appear in the virtual library, some method must be found to provide the author and publisher with a return on the on-line investment, one that doesn't damage existing sales. Can we find a way to bill for on-line usage intelligently, so that access to documents on-line generates revenues just as access to physical books does?

The answer seems to be yes. And it's a method that works not only for the on-line library, but for the providers of commercial databases. In particular, billing procedures are in the process of changing, so that we can be charged incrementally for services we actually use, rather than monolithically for access to features we may or may not need to draw upon. Electronic copyright protection schemes have begun to proliferate, usually involving software that establishes a connection between the owners of intellectual property and its users.[7] A copyright clearinghouse, for example, can keep track of when a particular text is displayed, copied, or downloaded; it can then charge a royalty for the use of that property, with the royalty being divided between publisher, author, and the clearinghouse itself. Thus Digimarc Corporation's "electronic watermark" system, which embeds a transparent code into a digital image, audio, or video file.

Use of the file results in appropriate payment being made to the holder of the copyright. By charging by the page or information unit, making the fees low but fair (and thus commensurate in some fashion with the cost of the printed counterpart), we begin to harness the power of our search engines to locate information in a universal context.

Passing the Cyberbuck

How serious is the prospect of microtransactions? Dutch software pioneer Digicash has partnered with Mark Twain Bank of St. Louis to set up so-called E-cash accounts that can be opened with real money and then used to buy things on-line. One purpose of E-cash is to allow the transfer of such microtransactions from any vendors who accept E-cash as payment. On another front, General Media International, the publisher of *Omni* and *Longevity* magazines, has taken both out of print circulation and into cyberspace-only editions, supported by microtransaction technology. San Francisco–based CyberCash Incorporation is working on an electronic coin service that allows game playing on-line in arcade-style format. And VISA International and MasterCard International have agreed on a secure electronic transactions standard that is eventually intended to support microtransactions.[8]

Another intriguing idea is called Clickshare, from Newshare. This Internet-based collection system can track when you access a particular document and charge your account a minor fee, with proceeds being distributed as appropriate. Meanwhile, Ted Nelson's

Xanadu project, an attempt to create a universal library of knowledge via hypertext, has originated the concept of "transcopyright." The latter breaks payment for particular parts of a work into so-called nanobucks—billionths of a dollar. Both Newshare and Xanadu are working with a productive concept, whether either becomes a cyberspace standard or not. The ability to charge tiny amounts of money via conventional credit card methods could be the driver that creates the true virtual library.

Canceling the Subscription

The subscription-based payment model used by the DIALOGs and Dow Jones News/Retrievals of this world is going to be undermined. The model of on-line research we'll all be able to use in a few years will work like this: When I need information about, say, corporate earnings in the energy sector, I'll run a search through any one of the numerous search engines on the Internet. I will either generate this search with a set of carefully constructed keywords, or I will be relatively loose with my language, asking the computer to "show me the latest corporate earnings posted by energy companies." The computer will produce a list of documents meeting my description, with appropriate links.

Now here's the key: The documents I will access may be located in databases or virtual libraries just about anywhere. They may be commercial in nature or, perhaps, freely available as government information or the work of private individuals. Whatever their source, those that require payment will be accessible without subscription. When I click on a link to call one of them up, I will trigger a billing mechanism that charges me only for the actual pages I read in the document I am accessing. If I click on another, I will pay for only the pages I read in it. Behind the scenes, the billing transaction will debit my credit card in whatever amount is accumulated during my data foray. The payment may have to be distributed among several different companies, and it may be divided into tiny amounts—microtransactions. But whether it's $.01 per page or $1.00 per page, I will be able to make the choice to see the document and pay for the use of it on-line.

The microtransaction model is a powerful way to look at information. In the context of the virtual library, it means that I can locate my copy of Plutarch's *Moralia* and run a search for the writer's views on dinner parties. I can enter certain keywords—*dinner*, perhaps, or *guests*, or a combination of the two using whatever connectors my search engine has implemented—and soon I will have, not the entire book on-line, but a specific segment of that book that meets my criteria. I can then read the chapter, or section of a chapter (perhaps only a paragraph), in question, possibly printing it out for later reference. Thus I have what I need from Plutarch and am billed for the actual usage. Let's say I read 1.38 pages at a cost of $.10 per page; I'm billed for $.138, which shows up as part of my credit card statement next month. The publisher is happy, as is the editor of the Plutarch edition I used, as is the company that facilitated the microtransaction.

But what's to prevent me from calling up the entire book on-screen and reading it there, thus hampering book sales in the stores? Nothing. If I choose to do so, I can read the entire 16 volumes of the *Moralia* on-line, paying a per-page cost that winds up equaling the cost of the printed volumes. But do I want to do this? I've yet to meet a person who has read an entire book on-line. Even the sharpest screen resolution hurts my eyes when I attempt extended reading. And although I am wed to my ThinkPad, a machine like this isn't something I want to curl up with in front of the fire. Why would I take it there, when a real book feels like a book, smells like a book, is browsable like a book, doesn't need recharging, and sits handsomely on my library shelves?

But let's say only the virtual book exists. What then? For example, I downloaded Howard Rheingold's *Tools for Thought: The People and Ideas of the Next Computer Revolution* (New York: Simon & Schuster, 1985) because the book had gone out of print, and its author placed it upon the World Wide Web once rights reverted to him (http://www.well.com/user/hlr/texts/tftindex.html). I found it so provocative that I decided to read it straight through. To do so, I printed out each chapter individually on my laser printer. I created, in other words, a physical book, the only kind of book that works for extended reading. But when I wanted to search through Eric Drexler's *Engines of Creation* (New York: Anchor Books, 1986) to locate a specific discussion of cell repair technology that could revolutionize medicine, I used the on-line version (http://reality.sgi.com/whitaker/EnginesOfCreation/). In the case of the Drexler book, I knew precisely what I wanted to read and could locate it through hypertext far faster than I could by paging through the printed volume (which existed not 10 feet away on my shelf), hoping I remembered approximately where I had read the material I was seeking. In this case, I would have paid if necessary (the site was free) for the quick access the on-line version provided, because the ability to search it is a value-added feature that can generate additional revenues for publishers farsighted enough to use it. The Drexler book's hyperlinks likewise made it easier to check glossary terms and run down the references I needed for research.

Make no mistake, the real and the virtual libraries require two different kinds of reading. The real book can be opened wherever we choose and leafed through; the computer screen, like the older papyrus rolls the codex book replaced, can only be scrolled, unless we choose to search it. But that search capability, and the concomitant ability to link to other text in the same file, provides a powerful new way of examining words. The point is, rather than fearing computers will replace books, we should understand that they're a natural complement to them. Publishers will not lose revenues because of on-line books; they will gain revenues, because the different libraries target entirely different audiences. One promotes traditional reading, a lengthy and leisurely pursuit. The other promotes scholarly, targeted, precise searching, homing in on specific knowledge.

The virtual library begins to merge with the real library when we offer access across the spectrum of published works without the need to subscribe to specific sites. But the downside to the microtransaction scheme must also be addressed. To consider it, let's return for a moment to the concept of fair use. As presently constituted, copyright law allows you to post a review of a book, quoting from it to make your point; this is not considered a violation of copyright. But an airtight microtransaction system *would* regard it as such; a digital watermark, for example, makes no distinction between the casual reader pulling down a chapter of a novel and the reviewer quoting that novel for the newspaper.

Could this enforcement of copyright across the board become an onerous burden to writers and reviewers? Perhaps. On a broader level, such payment requirements could put pressure on libraries and make educational use of computers prohibitively expensive. It's clear, then, that the fair use concept is in need of defense; any system of copyright that enables microtransactions must also provide a fair use escape mechanism that can distinguish between minor quoting and wholesale downloading. The specter of an Internet paralyzed by a set of fee schedules and collection processes is not a likable one, particularly given the Net's growth as a conduit of free, uncensored information. But the building of the virtual library cannot take place without adapting existing copyright protections to digital media. The last such attempt was made in 1976, and it is time to recognize the vast shift in retrieval methods that has occurred in the interval and to work toward a system that protects copyright but also encourages research.

Extending the microtransaction model into the realm of the library is inevitable. Enabling it will be increased bandwidth, as the Internet broadens its pipes and moves to high-speed copper-based telephony, satellite feeds, and cable television modems. We can imagine a virtual library where current titles are maintained through a robust system of microtransactions, while older books (those not currently in print, for example) are made available for free. The model benefits from the easy accessibility to resources that it offers, while traditional print libraries maintain their role as repositories of physical books. These books remain freely available for checkout, and they are not threatened by the existence of the networked virtual library, for the two libraries complement each other's strengths. If we accept the view that virtual books will coexist of necessity with their physical counterparts, we can answer the concern that the virtual library is creating a society of information-rich versus information-poor people. While a virtual library can't be created with full access to resources out of altruism alone, we have a social obligation to insist that traditional library holdings continue to exist for those without access to computers or the funds to pay for those virtual books that are fee-based.

Tomorrow's Web will be a mixture of free sites, still in the overwhelming majority, and sites that use some form of microtransaction to support the delivery of commercial information, all backed by on-line, targeted advertising. It will include in a progressively expanding fashion the traditional literature of the physical library, so that as bandwidth grows, we will be able to look forward to a future when we can access the card catalog and retrieve the titles we find on-line. Various models are possible; one is to do what Laura Fillmore's Open Book Systems is now experimenting with—surround the text with multimedia interactivity, offering the words for free while charging for access to the accompanying idea-stream of discussion areas, linked Web sites, and chat groups.[9] This may succeed with new titles, but who will have the time to create such links for the millions of volumes of earlier literature we hope to bring on-line as the virtual library begins to mirror the physical one? Perhaps a two-track system will develop, with new content being enhanced as the media allows and older works being accessible primarily as textual resources. Whatever the case, as the revenue stream from their Net activities grows, publishers will increase their commitment to two-track content, delivering both physical and on-line books, maximizing the potential of each.

Librarians, not programmers, are the key to the growth of the virtual library and the Internet at large. When I speak to people in the library community, I'm always surprised at the gloom that has settled upon these keepers of our cultural inheritance. They're not sure that their efforts are adaptable to the digital media, and unclear about how their current job descriptions translate into cyberspace. Instead of moving physical books, cataloging objects, hustling down research from indices and bibliographies, will they become something like data processors, sitting for long hours behind their computer screens, shipping virtual books around the planet at the speed of light?

My message to them is that the Internet is not a threat to traditional books any more than the airplane is a threat to the automobile. Each provides opportunities for significantly enriching the human experience; each can be a gateway into expanded knowledge and the productive use of information. I can do things with a hypertext book, by way of jumping between concepts, linking quickly to footnotes and glossaries, and exploring related information, that I can't do with a physical book. But I can do things with a physical book, like browsing productively, making serendipitous discoveries, reading beside the fireplace, that I can't do with a virtual book. As the two delivery mechanisms develop in parallel but distinct tracks, those who predict a paperless future are doomed to disappointment, but so too are their technophobic counterparts.

CHAPTER 7

Knowledge Assembly

Knowledge assembly is all about building perspective, and it happens through the accretion of unexpected insights.

In the dark days of the Iran hostage crisis in 1979–1980, I often turned to shortwave radio for information. As the presidential election neared, U.S. networks were reporting that a deal was in the works to free the hostages in time to save the flagging Carter campaign. I tuned my receiver to Radio Tehran to see if the Iranian position was softening, only to find that the deal, if indeed it was pending, was well concealed. The stream of propaganda continued unabated, mixed with martial calls to continue the revolution. And sure enough, the hostages weren't released until the day Carter left office.

Good information gathering is often a balancing act. In this case, Radio Tehran, a less than reliable source, provided an antidote to the usually more accurate Western media. But Tehran's declarations of victory over the United States, in turn, needed balancing by the Voice of America, which itself needed balanc-

195

ing by the BBC, an excellent news source, but one that, during the Falklands War in 1982, needed balancing from Radio Argentina Exterior, and so on. Even in those days, history had already become a multimedia exercise. All these radio stations could be checked against print sources like *The Washington Post* or *The New York Times*; the former balanced politically by *The Washington Times*, the latter by other dissident voices on the right, like the *National Review*. Television could bring photographs and live video of the drama, which could be explicated at length in feature articles and editorials. It's fascinating to speculate on how the Internet would have covered the hostage story.

We can view the Internet as yet another source in the ever rising torrent of journalistic chatter, or we can see it as a necessary filter that helps us get to the underlying issues. Used properly, networked information possesses unique advantages. It is searchable, so that a given issue can be dissected with a scalpel's precision, laid open to reveal its inner workings. It can be customized to reflect our particular needs. Moreover, its hypertextual nature connects with other information sources, allowing us to listen to opposing points of view and make informed decisions about their validity.

And its data sources are remarkably broad. The increasingly convergent nature of the Net provides access to archives from the world of broadcast media, such as databases of radio shows and, soon, television news reports, which we will be able to search for using keywords and replay as needed. Newspaper accounts can be read on-line and weighed against previous articles on the subject stored in the site's archives. Discussions by people directly affected by events can be monitored on the newsgroups and mailing lists. Meanwhile, customizable datafeeds of the kind we discuss in this chapter allow us to target a particular story and receive daily updates about its progress. Using these tools and evaluating the results is a process I call *knowledge assembly*.

Personalizing the News

Knowledge assembly begins on the Internet with a personal news service. By entering keywords that fit the topic you want to learn about, you can customize such a service to send breaking stories on that subject to you, either through electronic mail or via a World Wide Web site whose pages can be tailored for your use. An increasing number of these services are becoming available as publishers experiment with news delivery.

Having created a personal newsfeed, your second step is to locate and subscribe to newsgroups and mailing lists that deal with your subject. These offer a personal view of events; while they're often filled with opinion and hearsay, they do make it possible to understand what people affected by a news story are thinking, a key to understanding its significance. Newsgroups also provide newsfeeds of their own, such as the ClariNet service we'll examine in this chapter. As made available by many Internet service providers, ClariNet's clari newsgroups are broken into finely grained subtopics, allowing you to search for news in a focused way and update yourself daily or hourly. These groups tap the AP and Reuters newswires and act as a double check on your

Web-based newsfeed. Newsgroups are also helpful because messages in them frequently mention related resources, like Web sites with coverage of an ongoing story.

Step three is to search the Internet for background information. In the realm of hard news, the best place to start is by examining on-line newspapers and their archives; a search like this fills you in on the development of the story until now, often giving you a sequential listing of headlines and stories showing how the issue evolved. Other Internet options include using search engines to find sites related to the key players in a story, and to track down related sites that might provide valuable context for your work.

Step four is to pull together your remaining Internet news sources, which can be diverse indeed. Radio archives can turn up news stories that you can play using RealAudio. Even an interactive chat session can provide valuable clues for continuing the search, and don't forget that you can use e-mail to verify questionable information.

The fifth and final step in knowledge assembly is to move beyond the Internet to relate what you have found to nonnetworked sources of information. It is crucial that you do not overlook this step, for it is at this point that you place the story you are working on in the context of the wider world of news and information. Using the Net alone, you put blinders on events; you see only what you search for. A good newspaper can place the story within the context of other news; if the subject you are following appears not as a headline but on page 12, this itself tells you something. Library research likewise can uncover reams of data that has yet to be digitized. Television provides immediacy the Net lacks but, as we'll see, has serious shortcomings in terms of context.

Filling the Information Cache

Knowledge assembly is the ability to collect and evaluate both fact and opinion, ideally without bias. Knowledge assembly draws evidence from multiple sources, not just the World Wide Web; it mixes and distinguishes between hard journalism, editorial opinion, and personal viewpoints. The process accepts the assumption that the Internet will become one of the major players in news delivery in the twenty-first century, but it also recognizes the continuing power of the traditional media. Filling an information cache requires all your skills at content evaluation. Consider how many different sources I could use to research a story on the American aircraft industry. I would begin by setting up a personalized news service that would alert me to breaking stories. This is always the first step because events change quickly, and the speech made today, the report issued tomorrow, may place all your research in a different perspective. I would also join any mailing lists or newsgroups that focused on this topic. In this way, I would enable two different ways of looking at my subject. The traditional news-gathering organizations would be supplying me with news filtered through their editors, while the open nature of mailing lists and newsgroups would allow me to listen in on conversations about my topic. These might not be as authoritative, but they might point to valuable leads.

I would then run keywords through search engines to look for relevant sites, using search terms like *aircraft*, *industry*, *transportation*, and *airline*. I would be careful to consult multiple search engines, knowing that the databases of each vary, and that what turns up at one site may differ substantially from what I find at another. My searches would take me to home pages from major players like McDonnell Douglas and Boeing, and perhaps to industry reports available through brokerage house sites. I would scout through the resulting pages trying to identify which were the most reliable, following links to pages of related information. I would gather news stories from newspaper archives that discussed events materially affecting the aircraft industry. I would check audio archives for any radio discussion shows dealing with aviation. At the same time, I would continue to compare the material I found on-line with what I found in more traditional media, including television news and newspaper stories. As you'll see, one thing that differentiates the Internet from other forms of media is the contextual envelope surrounding it. On the Internet, I can link directly to related materials, while excluding items that don't connect to my subject matter. This is both good and bad; good in the sense that my search is focused, bad in that other news items often provide their own kind of context for an event. At times, only a print newspaper can deliver that context, by requiring you to page through it to see your story embedded in the rest of the day's news. And bearing in mind that most of the world's information has yet to be digitized, I would continue my research with trips to a physical library to consult reference books. But even here, the Internet would be valuable. I would use the Library of Congress on-line catalog to generate my list of sources.

The Internet demands a comprehensive, and necessarily skeptical, approach to information. There is no question that you can find material on-line that would otherwise be unavailable. But whether you're engaged in research on a report or business project or simply combing the news sites about a topical subject, you'll want to incorporate at least some of the methods outlined here. After a while, they will become second nature. True, casual reading requires a less disciplined approach, but you must continue to insist upon verifiability and linkages to the source when doing research, for while the Internet creates its own verification issues, it also provides the technology with which to solve them.

The Personal Newsfeed

Let's examine a news story that has set the world on its ear, both from within and without the Internet. On August 7, 1996, NASA announced that it had discovered what seemed to be microscopic fossils in a meteorite blown off Mars during some ancient catastrophe. Scientists at the NASA Johnson Space Center and Stanford University reported these findings at a news conference that previewed the team's report to the scientific community, which later appeared in the journal *Science*.[1] The supposed remains of the bacteria-like organisms found inside the Martian rock could be dated back some 3.6 billion years, leaving open the question of whether life exists on Mars today. And the team was exceedingly cautious about their findings. "We are not claiming that we have found life on Mars," said planetary scientist David McKay. "And we're not claiming that we have found the smoking gun, the absolute proof, of past life on Mars. We're just saying we have found a lot of pointers in that direction."

I first encountered this story not on the Internet but on television, when I heard Dan Rather's announcement on *CBS News* while I cooked dinner. The story received overwhelming attention and was hailed in some quarters as the defining moment of the twentieth century; in fact, reporter Cokie Roberts would describe it in exactly those terms the following Sunday on ABC's *This Week with David Brinkley.* Although I remained skeptical, as a lifelong believer in extraterrestrial life I nonetheless wanted to know more about how a rock from Mars could find its way to Earth in the first place, and how it could be reliably identified as Martian. Determined to learn more, I decided to apply the principles of knowledge assembly to the story, using the varied resources of the Internet and the other forms of media accessible to me.

The story was breaking daily, with updates from scientific teams all over the world. Thus I quickly implemented the first step in knowledge assembly, which is to create a personalized newsfeed to ensure that from this point on I didn't miss any new developments. Only when the personal newsfeed is established, quietly gathering information in the background as you work, can you turn back to conduct research on earlier materials that have crossed the Net. A newsfeed can come from many sources, for more and more companies are experimenting with delivering customized content, some on a subscription basis, others hoping to recoup their expenses through advertising. All of which points to how far we have come in the evolution of the term *news.*

In the early days of the Internet, news meant the various exchanges of inside information passed along by scientists and researchers engaged in a common project. The medium was electronic mail, later supplanted by electronic mailing lists. News took on a different slant with the arrival of the newsgroups (old network hands who speak of the news invariably refer to USENET), while electronic journals could also be considered news carriers, though, like mailing lists, they served a limited community of subscribers.

The second wave of news gathering occurred through the World Wide Web, which saw mainstream newspapers and print magazines appear in the electronic world. From modest beginnings on commercial information services, these offerings soon took advantage of the Web's graphical features and interactive links to provide an enhanced electronic equivalent of the print publication. The model was demand-based; you picked a site you wanted to visit and went there, entering its address in your browser. Once there, you browsed the various links looking for information, perhaps using a search tool provided by the publisher to help you find what you needed.

Both methods are innovative, especially for those who appreciate the ability to access information from their desktop that previously would have required a trip to newsstand or library. But neither takes advantage of the ability of the Internet to personalize information; neither exploits the ability of the microprocessor on your desktop to interact intelligently with the remote server to change the way news is presented. That breakthrough would come later, with the arrival of services designed to offer news in a format tailored for individual use. Coupling keyword searching with access to newspaper archives and personalized delivery mechanisms, these services took news distribution beyond browsing to offer pinpoint retrieval on demand.

The advantage? Consider what happens when we read news the conventional way. First of all, we're at the mercy of our newspaper's or magazine's publisher; whatever schedule the publishing company chooses is the one we must follow. As a demand-based medium, the Internet allows us to move to what we need when we need it, and provides significantly wider ability to choose between sources at a given moment. Second, traditional newspapers and magazines stack up; we fall behind in our reading and accumulate back issues we may intend to read but often can't find the time for. Personal news delivery allows us to cut through this clutter by acting as a clipping service. We can retrieve stories without effort and ensure that we don't miss out on significant news. Finally, user profiles are adjustable. We can modify them at will to track events according to our needs, letting the service retrieve and display this material.

Delivery services are diverse. They include electronic mail, through which some providers offer private newsfeeds and others interactive lists of topics that let you choose which stories you want to have sent to you. NewsPage, from Individual Incorporated (http://www.newspage.com/), for example, consults over 500 information sources on topics ranging from financial news and market analysis to banking, health, the high-tech industry, travel, and real estate. For a fee, you can set up a newsfeed that results in pointers to articles on your topic being delivered daily to your electronic mailbox. Scanning these pointers, you can choose any articles that you want to see and double-click to launch your Web browser, which will access the NewsPage site and display the story.

A variant of this approach is PointCast, from PointCast Incorporated (http://www.pointcast.com/), which delivers its newsfeed in screen-saver format; leave your computer idle for a predetermined time and a scrolling news ticker will pop up, with links to background information, including customized news, stock quotes, and weather. The software can be set to download information on a schedule of your choice.

Another take is to offer a personalized World Wide Web page, with links to specific news offerings that suit your needs. Ziff-Davis Interactive (http://www. zdnet.com/), for example, is a customized news service that taps information available in the various computer magazines the company produces. Having set your user profile using keywords, you can log on at any time to retrieve stories of interest. Netscape offers a similar service, tapping content from sources such as *The New York Times* and delivering it as personal Web pages (http://home.netscape.com/). Even search engines are getting into the act; the InfoSeek Personal Page (http://personal.infoseek.com/) sets up personalized news stories on politics, world news, sports, and stock market reports, all in the form of a custom-designed Web page.

Personalized news services also use older forms of Internet delivery—newsgroups for one. Services like ClariNet let you choose precise topics and retrieve daily updates through your newsreader or browser software. Mailing lists continue to be active news sources through specialized providers like EDUCOM, the Washington-based consortium on educational computing, which produces a newsletter called Edupage (http://educom.edu/web/edupage.html). *The Financial Times* (http://www.ft.com/) offers an e-mail service for readers whose travels may have caused them to miss significant events. Upon request, the paper will deliver a weekly summary of the news.

With all these options available and many more being implemented, the choice can be a difficult one. To make it, consider the kind of material accessed by each service. To follow the Mars story, for example, I elected to use NewsPage. I liked the fact that the service would send the news to me daily as an electronic mail message, with links to its Web site. What I would receive would be a synopsis of all the stories News-Page had gathered that fit my profile; I could then click on any of them to retrieve the full text. With over 25,000 pages of news moving through the NewsPage site every working day, my chances of tracking this breaking story seemed better here than anywhere else.

Setting up the profile, however, was not a day at the beach. The selection process involved creating a personal profile by selecting news topics, using the company's NewsPage Direct service. Over 600 information sources are available at this site, including major publications in each of the major topics covered by the search engine. But 2,500 topics can be found here in all, and the problem becomes one of choosing which is most likely to pull in the story you're after. Unlike standard keyword methods, News-Page wanted me to pick and choose among its menus of these topics, and some of them weren't obvious. Given a choice among major topics, like Telecommunications, Business Management, and Aerospace & Defense, it was clear that the latter would be the most likely choice for material on Mars, but subtopics were also subdivided with merciless precision. Which subtopic? New Technologies? Commercial Aviation and Space?

Here a lesson about knowledge assembly becomes blindingly clear. The Internet's lack of standardization requires you to combine resources to make such decisions. For example, most sites involved in the information business now include some kind of search engine as part of their package. At NewsPage, it's possible to run a search through the combined holdings at the site under a specific keyword. To determine which topics I should use in my personal profile, then, I ran a search under the keyword *mars*, quickly retrieving every story that mentioned Mars in even a peripheral way. I then checked each story to determine which topics News-Page had assigned it. It quickly became obvious that the topics to watch were Commercial Aviation & Space and, for reasons still not clear to me, Military Uses of Space. I was then able to move into the NewsPage Direct profile page and choose these topics to receive customized news.

Now I was in business; new stories about Mars appeared in my mailbox daily. When I ran the search engine, I pulled in stories from the previous two days about the Mars meteorite. These included a statement from Daniel S. Goldin, the NASA administrator who cautioned the world, "We are not talking about 'little green men.' " Another story came from Reuters, discussing how Mars had been described in the work of science fiction writers from H. G. Wells to Kim Stanley Robinson. A second Reuters story speculated on the future of NASA's Mars exploration, concluding that the process of sending unmanned probes to the planet, which already included 10 spacecraft scheduled over the next decade, would be accelerated. Finally, the M2 Presswire delivered an address for NASA's images of the meteorite. Looking at the site (http://rsd.gsfc.nasa.gov/marslife/), I found not only eerie photographs of what seemed to be tiny micro-fossils, but also the audio track of the NASA news conference announcing their discovery.

Clearly, knowledge assembly includes detective work. One source delivers numerous stories about your topic. Within one of these stories is embedded a Net address that takes you to a second wellspring of information which, in turn, contains links of its own. The hypertext methodology you use to navigate through Web pages is equally applicable to the process of knowledge building itself. Patience, which is what following hyperlinks requires, can pay off with unusual discoveries.

The Individual Voice

My customized newswire meant I would miss no significant events in the ongoing story of life on Mars. What I wanted now was to see what people were saying about these events and to keep my ear to the ground for further sources of information. This is step two in knowledge assembly: subscribing to relevant newsgroups and mailing lists. The USENET newsgroups, the Internet's ongoing conversations, are where this is done.

A newsgroup is the collective publication of its subscribers. Yet in this context, *subscriber* has a different connotation. To subscribe to the printed edition of *The New York Times*, you send in a check and receive the paper only so long as your account is current, whereas newsgroup subscriptions are free and are established merely by setting your software to receive the postings on that newsgroup. With thousands of newsgroups available, newsreader programs assume that you want to subscribe to none; it's up to you to go through the list of possibilities and pick any groups that interest you.

This in itself can be a daunting task, but you can run search terms against the list of newsgroups offered by your service provider, thus isolating those that might be of interest. In my case, I could call up my newsreader and run a search for the keyword *mars*, which turned up nothing, and the keyword *astro*, from which I hoped to uncover groups dealing with astronomical issues. And indeed, the latter uncovered sci.astro, which would become my main newsgroup source. It also uncovered alt.binaries.pictures. astro, a group from which I was able to download photographs of astronomical objects. Another group, alt.mars-life, had come into existence because of the NASA announcement (I read about it in a subsequent newsgroup posting), but I discovered that my service provider didn't yet carry that group. It's always a good idea to use your newsgroup software to check periodically for new newsgroups, because depending on your provider, you may see frequent additions to the list, particularly when a story has generated widespread interest.

The newsgroups I found, though, weren't the only place to turn for scientific and astronomical information. A search through the list of newsgroups made available by Interpath, my service provider, turned up a group called clari.tw.science + space, a group that listed news stories on space-related events. The clari groups are a different take on USENET news, in that they're based on hard news. The product of ClariNet Communications Corporation in San Jose, California, the ClariNet electronic news service delivers stories from United Press International and Reuters, including numerous features and columns on politics and entertainment, as well as financial information. A site that receives this USENET newsfeed from Clari-Net (and many providers make it available to their subscribers) can be used to monitor news events from hundreds of separate newsgroups, each containing a specific news topic. The effect is like that of a personal newswire, which you activate by subscribing to the appropriate newsgroup.

The group sci.space.news carried similar stories, including the transcript of the NASA briefing and a press release from the University of Florida on the possible source crater on Mars for the controversial meteorite. An August 7 story on clari.tw.science + space discussed the views of British scientists who had studied Earth life under extreme conditions of temperature and depth. Another story, from Reuters, interviewed Stanley Miller, a pioneer in the field of life's origins. In a 1953 experiment, Miller had re-created the atmosphere of the primordial Earth to discover that amino acids could be produced within it. "The origin of life," said Miller, "is a relatively easy thing."

Here we see a sharp distinction between the various types of newsgroups. The sci.astro group is typical in that it offers a medium for anyone to submit their thoughts, while the clari.tw.science + space and sci.space.news newsgroups are restricted to press releases and hard news. Both can be valuable sources of information, of course, but I find the conventional newsgroups helpful in that they offer a broad sampling of public opinion on an issue. They're also where new Internet sites devoted to your topic are frequently announced; I found many of the best Web sites on the Mars story by consulting them.

Looking at sci.astro, for example, I found that the Mars story had completely overrun all other discussions. Initial inquiries about exactly what NASA had said in its press conference were quickly answered with a posting of the transcript of the August 7 event. This soon led to questions regarding the meteorite itself: Was it possible that the analysis of the rock as Martian concealed a flaw, and that the fossil remains were actually terrestrial? A wide-ranging discussion of the methodology followed, which compared the composition of the meteorite with results sent back by the Viking landers on Mars. Pointers were also given to several different Web sites that had devoted attention to the Mars story. Possible mechanisms for getting a rock from Mars to Earth, along with considerable skepticism that this particular rock was indeed Martian, then ensued.

How to evaluate such messages? In the case of controversial events, we must proceed with caution. The newsgroups are places where violently held opinions can be exchanged, often in the form of arguments and delphic pronouncements from those committed to a single view of reality. The Mars story, which quickly filled the sci.astro newsgroup with numerous discussions (threads), encouraged postings from astronomers and NASA personnel. But it also encouraged several creationists to question whether the findings were consistent with the Bible, inspiring heated invective on both sides. One thread quickly degenerated into a battle between believers in evolution and religious fundamentalists who thought their views were under attack. Soon NASA's own credibility was under fire, as contributors brought up the so-called face on Mars, an anomalous formation that NASA photographed on an early orbital mission to the planet. Why, these people asked, was NASA making such a big deal about bacteria when there might be a lost civilization on Mars?

You can see how discussions like this can soon dominate the proceedings. Yet while the newsgroups can't often be accused of dispassionate analysis, their value for the news gatherer is immense. To understand the reaction of people across a broad spectrum of occupations and backgrounds to a major news story, nothing can serve better than a well-chosen newsgroup. There, people can publish their views without filtering by reporters or editing for network news time. What they have to say may not always be rational, but in some cases, it will suggest a viewpoint or an analysis that may not have been readily visible from reading more established sources of news. An intense debate about NASA's methodology in claiming the meteorite was indeed Martian led to useful analysis of the Viking results as well as theorizing about life on Earth having originated on Mars. The quality of postings in sci.astro varied considerably, but the issues debated helped me to look for answers when I turned to more targeted searching on the World Wide Web.

Nor are the newsgroups alone in delivering the individual voice. Mailing lists, like newsgroups, distribute the thoughts of subscribers, but through mailings to a mailbox rather than open newsgroup methods. Many mailing lists are searchable through archival sites, and an increasing number of these sites have become available on the Web. The trick is to locate a group that is germane to the topic you are considering. On the subject of astronomy and space science, I was able to track down a list called Earth and Sky, consisting of weekly transcripts of an astronomy program offered on radio by Deborah Byrd and Joel Block. I also found a list called NASAINFO, with information about space missions, and ASTRONOMY, a list devoted to amateur and professional astronomers. I located these and several other mailing lists at two Web sites that specialize in such lists (http://tile.net/ and http://www.neosoft.com/internet/paml/). All the lists were available for subscription by electronic mail, and several maintained a searchable Web site for ease of access with a browser.

The Network Database

Armed with a personal newsfeed, and having pulled up a chair at the ongoing discussion on newsgroups and mailing lists, my next step was to locate suitable Internet sites for archival work. This is step three in the knowledge assembly process: fleshing out the information gleaned from daily news sources and discussions, looking for the kind of context that will explain why these events are happening and how the Mars story continued to evolve. On a deeper level, I was also searching for understanding about how we would recognize extraterrestrial life and confirm its origin.

Such a search can be run from the top down (choosing, for example, a newspaper or television station's Web page and looking for material) or managed through a search engine, identifying keywords for the story in question. As this was a hard news item, I opted to try television first by checking CNN's Web site (http://cnn.com/), knowing that the company has put a strong emphasis on translating its content into the digital media. There I found a search engine that would let me enter keywords to trace previous stories, including transcripts of broadcasts, as well as audio and video from selected segments.

Using the keyword *mars*, I quickly pulled up 34 stories, ranging from a gallery of astronomical photographs to several stories speculating about life on the planet before the NASA results had been announced. On August 6, CNN ran a story anticipating the NASA news conference and followed it with a special report on the findings the next day. Taking advantage of the multimedia format, the August 7 story provided cross-section photographs of the NASA evidence, along with audio files supporting the story. One, from American University astronomer Richard Berendzen, saw the Mars evidence as "a long-lost discovery, a thing that astronomers have been looking for for decades." Astronomer Carl Sagan also provided commentary through a downloadable audio file.

As the story developed over the following days, it was easy to track, for the CNN Interactive search results were laid out in chronological order. Some were whimsical, some speculative: A British gambler had won $1,540 on the premise that life elsewhere in the universe would be discovered within the year. The views of skeptics were available, as were those of theologians, who tried to place the findings in a religious context. By August 10, CNN was discussing future NASA missions to Mars, again backing its Web story with photographs and links to background materials at NASA itself on the sources for the story. NASA's associate administrator, Wesley Huntress, was interviewed on the same day, while an August 12 story discussed theories on how life evolves and the conditions that would presumably have existed on an early Mars.

With everything from animations depicting the Martian surface and moving video showing a rotating Mars through the eyes of the Hubble Telescope, CNN Interactive had backed its story with considerable multimedia resources. It even offered a quiz for readers, and links to related newsgroups. But a good Web site is also one that provides links to resources beyond the original site. CNN listed links to a NASA computer that contains daily press briefings, the NASA home page—which itself contains substantial coverage of the story—and the on-line site of *Science*, the magazine in which the NASA findings were published. A thorough backgrounder on planetary research, including a Web page stuffed with Martian facts and images, was available through the Lunar and Planetary Observatory at the University of Tucson, while *The New Scientist*'s coverage of the story involved a major feature on-line at its Web site. CNN was also lighthearted enough to set up links to science fiction stories about Mars available on-line, and a page devoted to Gustav Holst's *The Planets Suite.*

Hypertext leads from one resource to another in a progression of authoritative knowledge building. In this case, I relied upon CNN's known expertise at news gathering to act as an information filter, thus isolating sites I knew would be useful. But I had also used a newsgroup posting in the sci.astro newsgroup to home in on a final site, a superb feature from the Federation of American Scientists that appeared almost immediately after the NASA results were announced and offered a sequential set of news stories about the topic (http://www.fas.org/mars/). By checking there every day, I could find any stories that had slipped through my news-gathering service and verify that I was up to date.

For the sake of completeness, I also wanted to check out a major newspaper site. *The Washington Post* seemed the logical candidate. Its site (http://www.washingtonpost.com/) includes, in addition to features and other materials from the daily paper, a search engine that provides archival news, as well as a search engine for the stories that have moved across the AP newswire. Using the *Post*, I was able to pull up stories that treated the subject in detail, including a major feature by the paper's Kathy Sawyer called "Pushing the Boundaries of the Cosmic and the Microscopic," along with a more offbeat view from Art Buchwald. The AP newswire search yielded a helpful chronology of AP coverage. By the time I was through with both CNN Interactive and *The Washington Post*'s Web pages, I had a solid cache of material.

The Web pages I visited on my data hunt led me to numerous linked sites at other locations. In each case, the links could be considered significant, in that they bore the imprimatur of recognized news-gathering agencies. But for other sites, I also moved in my third step to search engines, using both AltaVista and InfoSeek. Choosing the appropriate search strategy uncovered many of the same sites that I found by examining CNN and the *Post*, making the point that Internet searches ultimately circle around the same core of material. But my search engine work also uncovered such things as a site specializing in using radio to communicate with extraterrestrial civilizations (http://www.seti-inst.edu/), a NASA-provided atlas of Mars (http://fi-www.arc.nasa.gov/), and a discussion of misconceptions about life on Mars since the earliest days of observing the planet (http://www.physics.sfsu.edu/asp/tnl/25/25.html). My most unusual find: an audio file of Orson Welles' famous *War of the Worlds* radio broadcast in 1938 (http://www.waroftheworlds.com/), made available on Halloween 1996.

By this point, information overload had set in, its surest symptom being the repetition of key sites on any new pages I ventured into. Indeed, the AltaVista search engine flagged some 30,000 entries under my original search coupling the keyword *mars* with *fossil*. I was forced to develop a tighter keyword strategy that narrowed my results to a manageable field. Several of these sites were not available through linkages on any of the other Web pages I consulted, driving home the point that knowledge assembly requires repeated attacks at the worldwide information horde, plus a willingness to separate out types of content. Again the caveat: Content evaluation is critical in distinguishing between filtered, edited news, and personal opinion, not to mention propaganda. Having made a sweep through the most authoritative sources I could find, I felt it was time to move on to other forms of knowledge assembly.

The Merger of the Media

We must always be alert for multimedia information, which can place a different spin on facts we already have learned. This is step four in knowledge assembly. The Internet is rapidly incorporating reporting elements from audio and video news-gathering sources; indeed, CNN Interactive was a highlight of my early investigations into the Mars story. What makes the Internet particularly attractive in mixed-media terms, however, is that it allows us to search archives of such materials. A radio show that would otherwise be broadcast and forgotten is available for listening by downloading the right software and clicking the mouse.

My first check for an audio/video archive took me to the PBS Online page (http://www.pbs.org/), a frequent stop when I need audio materials or transcripts of television programming. The Mars story was obviously significant enough to have gathered considerable national attention, as I had learned when I saw it handled as a lead story on the *CBS Evening News*. On the PBS page, I was able to link to the Online News-hour, where a keyword search pulled up a background page on Mars. Entitled "Clues from the Red Planet," it was in the form of an interview with Stanford chemistry professor Richard Zare and NASA associate administrator Wesley Huntress. The interview was in text form, but the page contained links to a RealAudio file of NASA's press conference itself, a collection of Mars photographs, and a second transcript collecting views from major players in the drama.

I decided to capture the original sound of the news story as it broke, so I moved to the RealAudio site (http://www.realaudio.com/), where ABC News maintains its own archives. Stories are categorized by date; by choosing August 6, I found the story on the 3:00 P.M. (Pacific time) broadcast, which led off with a quote from an unnamed scientist calling it "one of the biggest discoveries ever," and quickly segued into an audio clip from the movie *Independence Day*, which deals with an alien invasion of the Earth. Since the networks couldn't resist juxtaposing scientific talk with science fiction, I moved around at the Real-Audio site to examine an archive of radio shows from National Public Radio. Its August 7 lineup was considerably more detailed, including a report from Joe Palca laying out the evidence with the help of several interviews, and clips from President Clinton's remarks on Martian life. Palca's report laid out alternative explanations for the findings and the reasons why NASA believes they are unlikely.

The NPR archive also contained a collection of the network's *Science Friday* shows, the August 9 edition of which contained a lengthy discussion between host Ira Flatow and renowned scientist Frank Drake, one of the pioneers in the attempt to find intelligent signals in radio waves from outer space. Flatow was also joined by J. William Schopf, the director of the Center for the Study of Evolution and the Origin of Life at UCLA, who has emerged as one of the primary critics of NASA's findings. This almost hour-long show was perhaps the most detailed coverage of the Mars story I was able to uncover anywhere. It included major questions about NASA's work, including unresolved issues regarding whether the chemical composition of the Martian meteorite and the structures within could have been explained by natural processes other than life.

Knowledge assembly is all about building perspective, and it happens through the accretion of unexpected insights. Thus I found a third NPR story to be compelling. It was an interview, again playable through the RealAudio software, with Krister Stendahl, a bishop of the Church of Sweden and the former dean of Harvard Divinity School, discussing the theological implications of Martian life. Bishop Stendahl's view found no contradiction between Christian teachings and the spread of life throughout the universe. "If there is life, if that were the truth," the Bishop said, "God would be bigger than we thought, the universe would be more marvelous than we thought, and we would be living in a time much like that of Copernicus." Just as Copernicus understood that the Earth was not at the universe's center, so the Mars discovery tugs at our sense of place today.

Likewise, juggling perspectives is what our experience of media is all about. And the media are inescapably changed by their presence on a worldwide digital network. Consider another medium: conversation as expressed through live text. Conversation is at the far pole of the news picture; it is the most personal form of information gathering, yet it can be the most significant when we have isolated those people whose conversation reliably leads to knowledge. A conversation is a perspective-switcher; it compels us to examine our own viewpoints and measure them against any information we've gained by talking to our companion. We judge conversations by our measure of the participants. If I know you and have learned from you in the past, I value your thoughts on the possibility of life on Mars and take seriously your suggestions about its likelihood. If I don't know you, I discount what you say unless it is strikingly expressed and clearly backed with facts. In the absence of background knowledge of your character and education, I can form judgments based only on what I hear at the moment.

But the on-line chat is conversation without context. Indeed, the Internet's capabilities for providing background in this mode are slight. The most common form of chatting consists of people typing to each other; I type something in the field on my screen and press the Return key to send it. My message is seen by everyone else who is on the same "channel." Each of these people in turn has the ability to respond, his or her own messages appearing as a stream of consciousness flashing pixel by pixel as it is created on-line.

Chatting, like any Internet activity, requires software, a client program that puts the operation in some kind of order and provides pull-down menus and an interface that sorts out the complicated operations going on behind the scenes. Think of chatting in terms not unlike television: Individual conversations, consisting of the talk streaming through data packets between two or more people, are created around particular subjects. Anyone can set up a channel, and, as with newsgroups, you can join the channel of your choice. Moving about between channels, you sample topics until you find the one you want to participate in. Despite their subject matter, some channels are populated by people engaged in serious discussion; others seem inscrutable, if not pointless.

Chat inevitably puts you into present tense; words appear magically on your screen, followed by a jumble of others. Long periods of inactivity give way to machine-gun bursts of talk. The language is tightly constricted; sentences are punctuated with smiley faces and abbreviations; verbs are missing. This is the argot of the chat room, developed for a medium where ideas surface, submerge, shift incomprehensibly, and blend into jokes, drown beneath puns, rocket off on inexplicable tangents.

On the Undernet chat server in Ljubljana, Slovenia, I encountered a channel where Mars was being discussed. Perspectives from 27 people sprinkled the screen, for no one speaks in lengthy sentences while chatting. A Pakistani teacher called for a manned mission to Mars. The United States, he thought, had abandoned its space program. "Why waste the money?" countered the disembodied type of someone called Cage (names, or "handles," change freely in chat rooms), but that brought a strong response from Stan16, a Canadian. "We should go because people need to explore."

Chat is perhaps the least valuable of your knowledge assembly options, and despite the efforts of those who see its interactivity as a new form of community building,[2] it is unlikely to offer more than peripheral value to your work. In this case, repeated requests for that information brought nothing initially; the conversation drifted into a trip one of the participants was planning to take to Australia, which then turned into comments on how difficult and slow the service was this morning. But then another message broke through on the Mars story. I was told to check the *Albuquerque Journal* opinion page on-line for a relevant article. The gradual breakdown of the conversation, endlessly regrouping, and reinventing itself, propelled me back to my Web browser, where I ran a search for the *Journal* and found it (http://www. abqjournal.com/). There, a story by John Fleck cast doubt on the NASA findings. "The Martian meteorite in which NASA scientists say they found signs of life lacks one of the key chemical signatures of biological activity, according to University of New Mexico scientists who have studied the same meteorite for the past two years. While not directly contradicting the NASA scientists' work because of differences in the way the researchers studied the meteorite, the UNM group provided the first publicly available check on whether the NASA team is right, according to an independent expert familiar with the work."[3]

Thus the forms of media merge. A tip from someone I will never meet led me to a source I hadn't considered for an opinion about an issue I discussed in a chat room. And that source led me to a story I had missed, pointing to the fact that an occasional sweep through the chat channels may pay an unexpected dividend.

Electronic mail can perform many of the same functions. Unlike chat, mail used well can be a reflective medium. My understanding of the Kobe earthquake that devastated Japan in 1995 was powerfully influenced by electronic mail I received from the site, backed by accounts of the destruction I read on various USENET newsgroups. A lengthy electronic mail message about the assassination of Israel's prime minister Yitzhak Rabin was widely circulated on the newsgroups; it provided an eyewitness account of Israel's mourning. No one form of media could have conveyed in so striking a way what was happening, yet the complete experience involved television, radio, newspapers, and computers. Just as the news we retrieve in the future will inevitably come to be a conglomeration of multiple media types blending seamlessly through digitization.

Yet even converging forms of media maintain their differences. In media talk, convergence means blending content from the Internet with multimedia materials from sources as diverse as print, CD-ROM, radio, and television. It's the conflation of the computer, telephone, and television, driven by the coming growth in available bandwidth to include full-motion, full-screen video. But distinctions remain despite the delivery mechanism. If I access the latest news about Mars from a physical copy of *The Washington Post* or through the on-line version, I am reading the same content; what I do that is different is to add the new possibilities offered by the on-line format to that content. The dynamics of writing for the newspaper don't change, but the dynamics of editing for the reader do, revealing links and suggesting sources.

Mixing media may be called convergence, archiving, or repackaging, but whatever the term, each form of media carries the same constraints about how information is presented. The information consumer must weigh source, probable audience, and reliability. No medium is so complete that it can't be complemented by another.

Contextualizing the Internet

The reality, then, is that knowledge assembly depends critically upon other forms of media for inclusiveness; using these is step five in knowledge assembly. We profit from casting our nets widely, for the broadcast media operate under different assumptions than the Internet and thus provide their own perspective. And let's not forget that traditional print publications offer some powerful benefits as well.

Consider how television changes our view of the news. I can watch correspondents reporting from a NASA news conference and see the photographs of odd structures within a rock that scientists say is from Mars. CNN shows me images from Viking Mars landers and the Hubble Space Telescope. I watch interviews with leading scientists, and hear the reaction of skeptics, even as I see President Clinton reacting to news of the discovery and announcing the need for a summit to discuss space issues.

But I would argue that the impact of television isn't primarily visual. Yes, we see events, sometimes as they happen, but more often what we see is a journalist standing in front of an event, delivering a story that could as easily have been shot in the studio. What television does deliver is packaging, the grouping of fragmented, often isolated materials and their editing into a single, cohesive unit. The nightly news is an utter distillation of the events of the day as seen through the collected reports of correspondents around the world. Strip out the commercials and you wind up with some 22 minutes of airtime devoted to the entire globe's affairs. The producers have condensed what they see as the major news stories and, usually, a "soft news" feature—a profile of an interesting person or analysis of an issue—into a readily accessible package. The widely followed two-minute rule keeps all stories save war and major disasters under two minutes in length, hoping to still the hand that is reaching for the remote control to switch channels.

Is the Internet a "better" way to retrieve the news? Because it delivers content in user-specified ways, the Net does give us greater control over what we see when, but we lose the insistent "tapping on the shoulder" that we feel when one television network after another tells us that something is important. Television journalism is packaged news; it's always there, at the same time every day, with the same reporters and anchorpeople providing continuity. In the case of Mars, television news picks up the threads from last night's broadcast and reminds me of the four-pronged nature of the evidence of life and the various questions they raise. The television account is a reminder of what its editors think is important—mixed with the inanities of mass-market advertising: Martian craters and antacids; family dinners amidst the alien stone.

Fixation on a single media type is common with television; after all, it's the primary source of news for millions of people around the globe. But what it delivers in focus it loses in depth. Each news story, tightly compressed to fit time allotments and edited into short polemical statements, is a misleadingly simplistic look at complicated issues, which is why science fiction and science fact mingled so freely in its coverage of Mars. But cable television points toward a convergence with computer networking. We have tens of thousands of newsgroups and discussion areas on the Internet, not to mention millions of World Wide Web pages from thousands upon thousands of sources. Cable television, even via some of the new satellite services, can't equal that variety, but 150 channels do point to specialization, a process that has brought us CNN, C-SPAN, and Headline News, among others, and that will continue to generate news channels for the foreseeable future. A CNN can focus full-time on a news story if events warrant. Headline News at 8:00 or 10:00 P.M. can be supplanted by special reports; we all remember when CNN's coverage of the Gulf War brought events into our living rooms with a clarity and immediacy the medium had never before been able to create.

Shorn of the need to compress news events into the mind-numbing snippets of the 30-minute newscast, a cable television channel, if it has the resources, can provide play-by-play coverage of breaking events. We are then limited only by the position of the camera and the knowledge of the reporter; we see what the camera sees and hear the accounts given us by witnesses to the event. The television's eyes and ears complement what we find on the Internet, whose newsgroups can provide a parallel sense of immediacy. As the Internet spreads into the population at large, its ability to carry the thoughts of the average person increases. The difference between it and television now becomes one of interactivity, the ability of the viewer to become directly involved in the events of the moment. For that we need the Internet and the World Wide Web.

A print publication provides the contextualization that television lacks. The August 19 issue of *Time* ran the Mars story with a portion of the cover devoted to it. The "Life on Mars" spread included a diagram explaining how the meteorite might have found its way to Earth following an asteroid impact on Mars, as well as photographs of the worm-shaped structures believed to be Martian fossils. Leon Jaroff wrote the lead story, which couldn't resist its own science fiction clichés, including a movie poster from an Abott and Costello film. But the story also discussed the issues in depth, referring frequently to William Schopf's cautionary statements and considering the view of Mars through history, from H. G. Wells to Percival Lowell. Sidebars from other writers analyzed the theory of panspermia, which suggests that life spreads through biological seeds that are found throughout space, and NASA's next missions to Mars itself.

I could also read the Mars story via Time on-line at the Pathfinder site (http://pathfinder.com/). There, I found articles on the base story, explaining what NASA had discovered and discussing the implications of the finding for planetary research, as well as NASA's government funding. Full coverage of the skeptics' views, including those of astronomer Carl Sagan, found a voice here, and the issue could be debated in the site's bulletin boards, which provided a newsgroup-style discussion area.

All these articles were linked on the Web edition of *Time*'s coverage, but the overall effect was quite different in the physical magazine. While Mars had a spot on the issue's cover, the main cover photograph was of the Republican presidential ticket, a beaming Dole and Kemp. The big story that week, at least in *Time*'s view, was clearly the outcome of the Republican convention, with the entire center of the magazine taken up with an analysis of Dole's prospects, an analysis of Dole the man, and a feature on Jack Kemp's life. After a retrospective on Ronald Reagan and a study of the Republican Party in turmoil, *Time* had devoted 29 pages to the presidential race, as opposed to 8 pages on Mars. And, of course, the print magazine included the usual book and movie reviews, letters from readers, and columns from its regular writers. *Time* discussed the bombing at the Olympics in Atlanta, pondered the fortunes of baseball, and devoted a page to the career of Patsy Cline.

Many of these articles were likewise available in the on-line edition, but what stood out as I read the physical magazine was their context. On-line, I read targeted information; my search at the Pathfinder site had linked the articles about Mars together so that I could quickly move between them, ignoring all else. In my easy chair, I created my own hyperlinks by paging through the paper version of the magazine. The context surrounding the Mars story placed these events in the broader spectrum of history; it also provided the kind of linkage that would explain how the citizens of planet Earth might react to the discovery of life on another world. Intuition played into this, as did my own sense of history and the inexorability of scientific exploration. But I found my view shaped by the contextualization of both Web and printed newspaper. The true multimedia experience of radio, newspaper, computer network, television, and talk is the creation of one's own linkages through the hypermedia experience of being alive.

CHAPTER

A Future for the Digitally Literate

It's just possible that extended and highly developed virtual environments may offer us clues as we attempt to master the critical issues of living together in a physical world that is running out of resources and facing shortages in key areas of skill and education.

In the malleable world of cyberspace, today's breakthrough is tomorrow's anachronism; events move at speeds dictated by processor power and the human imagination, creating technological wunderkinder whose half-lives are measured in weeks, if not days. And I wonder: If things change this fast, is there any point in talking about the Net's future? Even armed with the tools of knowledge assembly, the Internet itself is a difficult subject to follow. I know this from my own work. On a typical day, I run sweeps through site after site, hoping to keep up with what is happening on the Net. I find myself fighting for focus, trying to see the story whole. New software tweaks existing ideas, pushing digital multimedia to its limits. Chip speeds accelerate; memory swells. Corporate take-overs alter the business map.

But if we can't always keep up with the specifics of Internet change, the core competencies of digital literacy remain viable. Technologies shift, but if you remember that knowledge assembly, Internet searching, hypertextual navigation, and content evaluation are all methods rather than specific hardware or software products, you will be able to apply them to the Net of tomorrow. New developments should be seen in perspective. If a revolutionary program advances audio quality to unheard-of levels, it will not change our use of audio in knowledge assembly; it will only make the listening experience easier and more enjoyable. The latest browser may incorporate a virtual reality breakthrough or links to a revolutionary search engine, but the issues it creates remain the same: How do we find, verify, and incorporate content in our work?

Invariably, the competencies we bring to bear on Net content can be broadened to address the developing technologies that will change the shape of our on-line experience, for digital literacy is the logical extension of literacy itself, just as hypertext is an extension of the traditional reading experience. We can approach Internet change as we do any other breaking story—by applying the methods outlined in this book to build and analyze content. As with any research effort, we must separate commercial hype from substance, rumor from fact, but this has always been a core Internet skill. If there is one certainty in the future of cyberspace, it's that onrushing technologies will compel us to sharpen our use of these knowledge-gathering tools on a continual basis.

Of Standards and Markets

The Web these new technologies explore would never have developed without the creation of standards that allowed people around the globe to position content within it. But commerce drives innovation on today's Net, and those companies that wait for formal standards to emerge will quickly lag the field. The high-tech warfare at the Internet's core will benefit desktop users by offering greater choice, freeing us from the need to make expensive purchases before examining major products, allowing us to compare and contrast programs, and punishing developers whose offerings fail to keep up. Breakthrough products and expensive misfires will litter the landscape.

For the line between standards and products is becoming hopelessly blurred. As competing Internet browsers battle for supremacy and new releases are injected into the data stream on an almost monthly basis, products define standards rather than vice versa. The result: an intensified pace of development as rival software houses fight for marketshare. For the end user, this development means a bewildering assault of competing programs incorporating experimental features and proprietary tools. We may expect the pace of change to accelerate even as the large corporations create worrisome issues about their products by treating the Net like a private fiefdom.

Changes in the HyperText Markup Language (HTML) that underpins the World Wide Web are already indicative of the change. Netscape Corporation, capitalizing on the Web's expansion, decided that its own extensions to HTML could be ratified by users rather than by standards-setting committees.

The result was an ever advancing set of changes to the Netscape Navigator browser. Netscape version 1.1, for example, added support for tables, which allowed the designer to display both graphics and text in columnar form. Netscape 2.0 added frames, which made it possible to navigate a Web site while maintaining a table of contents on-screen, a powerful incentive to organize confusing hyperlinks. The company built compatibility with Sun Microsystems' Java language into the same release, a bow to the Net's first programming language, but many of its changes were in fact de facto standards for the rest of cyberspace. Sites using them could be properly viewed only through the Netscape browser.

The process was not without its critics, for the Internet has always been universal in its application. A pivotal factor in the Net's growth has been its ability to connect different kinds of computers, so that we wouldn't be limited to specific manufacturers or software developers when using it. Proprietary standards create a tension between that openness and the push to corner market share. Smaller companies find it difficult to compete without the latest features; after all, when a Netscape can boast 80 percent of the market, its weight in determining what users see is substantial. On the other hand, a Netscape or a Microsoft can create an Internet-wide standard overnight due to that same clout, which can lead to technological breakthroughs and better products. The balance between coercion and innovation is a treacherous one.

The distribution process has similarly accelerated. The rush to bring products to the marketplace will see companies driving early versions of their programs onto their Web sites for evaluative downloads.

Other companies will be forced to follow the Netscape model, bypassing conventional channels of software distribution to reach the customer as quickly as possible. Surely the day is coming when we download most of our new software—not just our Internet programs—from Web sites, automatically updating them with the latest revisions whenever we access the company's home page. The Net thus takes on still more aspects of an ecosystem, tweaking the client programs that access it, tuning our connections in a distributed software evolution.

But software development in hyperdrive shouldn't obscure a core Net competency—the ability to fine-tune content through customized software. In fact, ever more sophisticated browsers and related tools will offer us enhanced capabilities to personalize our operating environments, retrieving the news we need when we need it. We will see software improvements that help us sort and catalog the material we find in our Net explorations, and we'll continue to use targeted content provided by an increasing number of publishers, especially our newspapers, as we engage in the necessary process of knowledge assembly. Sheer market pressure should keep the improvements in this technology cheap and readily available over the Net.

Agents and Intelligence

While the ability to search will thus remain a key Internet competency, how you run the search will change. Imagine you are tracking the ongoing hunt for peace in the Middle East. As you compose words on-screen, a software "agent" is active on the Internet examining Web sites. Having made multiple sweeps through the various search engines, the agent knows to look only for sites that have gone on-line since your last foray on the Net. Targeting these, it looks for select keywords, basing its search pattern not only on the terms you give it—say, "israel," "arafat," "palestine"—but also on words that have appeared frequently on sites to which you keep returning. The document you're composing in your word processor may suggest keywords as you compose your argument, for the agent can scan relevant materials looking for patterns in your writing. Perhaps you'll leave the agent out on the Net when you stop work for the day. Unlike you, the agent can keep searching all night long to monitor developments; you can review its results over your morning coffee.

An agent like this automates the search process; it's a digital tool that can locate information, bring it back, sort and catalog it, and even assist in your analysis. But more significantly, software agents of the sort now being contemplated will "learn" from their experience. Detecting patterns in your work, themes that interest you, or concepts to which you return, the agent will adapt by strengthening its searching on those parameters, while abandoning less productive channels of inquiry. Theoretically, a good agent should be able to track down things you may not have realized you needed. In doing so, the agent has analyzed what you do (as opposed to what you think you do), and has sculpted its search strategy accordingly.

Already we've examined the earliest examples of agents, tools that in their various ways attempt to customize our search operations. Many of the search engines now available allow customized searching or generate personal news pages, while services like PointCast or NewsPage allow us to set up filters against which their database is run. The true agent, however, is more personal still; in the future, it will reside on our machines, becoming one of the essential software tools that link us to the Net. Ultimately, it becomes the hinge that connects our various applications, binding the information in word processor files to database records and Net-based research sites. Agents reflect a changing relationship between individual and machine. The computer has been successful insofar as it has allowed us to commit intensive tasks, particularly in terms of number crunching, to its processors. Tomorrow's desktop machine will be powerful enough to reproduce human behaviors, using heuristic algorithms to mimic our intellectual habits and research patterns. While content verification will remain the domain of the researcher, content exploration will increasingly be managed by digital means. This expansion of computer power grows by necessity out of the stunning surge in available data. If it is true, as George Gilder says, that the amount of raw data will increase by a factor of 19 between the years 1990 and 2000, then researchers will have no choice but to automate their explorations.[1]

Agents are challenging because they seem to point to a change in the way we find information. But in fact, agent software simply takes existing technology and extends it. The issues of content verification that so dominate Web researchers today remain emphatically in force, whether the content we've downloaded comes from our own hunt through a Web site or from a list retrieved by an agent. The agent, much like today's search engines with their relevancy rankings, can only make informed guesses as to what we need. Even the most sophisticated agent may misinterpret our preferences, retrieving information that's wide of the mark. With agents, as with other kinds of searching, it will take experience and experiment to see how satisfactorily a particular product works, and how far it should be trusted to deliver useful content.

Caffeinating the Web

How that content is displayed on your screen is also undergoing change. Consider what happens when you click on a hyperlink to call up a Web page. The HyperText Transport Protocol responds by downloading information to your computer, where your Web browser interprets and displays it. The process, once it begins, is set up as a "transaction"; when it has taken place, the content on your screen is fixed. To catch any subsequent updates, you need to download the page again, and that second download is likewise a one-time operation. This process contrasts sharply with television or radio, where content is in a process of continual flux. A sitcom or talk show can be interrupted by a news flash, which can update itself as the story unfolds.

Think of the early Web as a series of snapshots that you paste into a flexible computer-generated scrapbook. Yes, the scrapbook can be updated as you choose with additional pictures and text, but the material you're looking at won't change before your eyes—which makes a particular category of content unavailable to you. That Web—the one that remained in place until, roughly, mid-1996—could not provide you with breaking news, updated sports scores, or stock prices, nor could it alert you to an infusion of content that occurred after you accessed the site you were examining.

But we're moving toward a model of Internet content that is more active than before, one with parallels to and yet significant differences from broadcast media like television. And whether you get your Internet connection over a telephone line, a satellite feed, or a cable television hookup, you'll be tapping a source of live, rather than canned, content. One way to do this is to use scripting, which means viewing the Internet as a programming platform. Just as Basic or Pascal can be used to create simple programs on your computer, it should be possible to use a network computer language to perform certain actions on the Internet. The language that has received the most attention in this regard is called Java. Developed by Sun Microsystems, Java lets you run computer programs through your Web browser. A Java-enabled site features Web pages from which you can download tiny programs called *applets* to your machine; these then run on your machine, providing the ability to update information on the fly, as well as to add interesting visual effects like ticker tapes and animated diagrams to your screen. Java-enabled browsers—both Microsoft Internet Explorer and Netscape are so enabled—have become de rigueur for the display of the latest Internet content.

Sun Microsystems' home page offers an illustration of Java at work. The URL is http://www.sun.com/, where you will find, among other things, a link to a Java-enabled page that provides the same information found on the regular home page, but in a somewhat livelier format. Images take on ambulatory life; a figure of a skyscraper flashes like a neon sign, while text scrolls across the screen under it, giving the effect of a news ticker updating you on Sun's systems. Icons can be static, or they can suddenly swirl into motion, changing texture and shape under the influence of Java.

All of which is fun to watch, and a good deal livelier than the traditional home page. But Java applications are also becoming more complex. Companies are developing real-time spreadsheets that can connect to live datafeeds (Applix); others are working on Web authoring tools (FutureTense), software development programs (PostModern Computing), and updatable stock graphing (Bulletproof). You can perform a dissection on a digital human body (http://www. npac.syr.edu/projects/vishuman/) or explore an interactive atlas (http://www.mapquest.com/). The Java Applet Rating Service (JARS) directory (http:// www.jars.com/) is a good place for sampling what Java has to offer today.

And while Java is first out of the gate with this kind of network scripting technology, Microsoft is active as well; its Visual Basic language is made to order to compete with Java for a share of the real-time Web market. Indeed, the fact that Microsoft considers a lively Web to be crucial is evidenced by its ActiveX technology, which is being built into the latest generations of Internet Explorer. An ActiveX-enabled browser can run Java applets, but it can also support Visual Basic applications that interact with Microsoft software, tightening the link between what you do on your machine and what you do on the Internet. Shockwave for Director, from MacroMedia, is another take on the situation; its capabilities as an add-on to a network browser bring a wide range of animation and other visual-effects tools to Web pages.

What the active Web page provides is not necessarily new content but the ability to monitor *changing* content, as well as to interact in richer ways with
the site, thus broadening the Net's participatory quality. But in a world where information is updated by
the second, content evaluation remains decisive. The
"live" Internet emphasizes the importance of examining the source and weighing the information against
other resources, all part of the critical approach to Net
content that we use when engaged in the process of
knowledge assembly. Rapid updates place the burden
upon the user as never before to examine content
with skepticism until it can be verified.

The Internet as Operating System

A live Internet also affects the balance of power in the
operating-system wars that have defined computing's
last decade. Apple Macintosh or Microsoft Windows?
OS/2 or UNIX? Such questions have dominated desktop computing since the earliest days, when an operating system called CP/M was the state of the art, and
Microsoft was just beginning to work with IBM to
make MS-DOS the standard for the IBM PC. Today,
despite consolidation thanks to Windows 95, operating system complexity remains an issue. Earlier versions of Windows are still common, while Mac and
OS/2 users retain a relatively small but robust market
share. The animated Web page hints at a changing
relationship between our desktop computers and the
external world of connected machines in that it
deemphasizes the importance of the local operating
system.

For Java aims at platform-independence; programs written for it should be able to run on any kind of computer, in sharp contrast to conventional software. I can't run Microsoft's Word for Windows on my Power Mac; I have to run the Macintosh-specific version of the software to use it. Nor can I get Anarchie, a powerful FTP and archie client for the Mac, to run on my ThinkPad, under either Windows or OS/2. But a Java application—and, by extension, any software developed under the same ground rules—will be able to run on any of these machines. It's conceivable that creating a universal standard for network software through a commonly used scripting language could change the way we distribute our basic computer tools, by which I mean the large programs like word processors, spreadsheets, and databases that provide so much of our experience of the machine. This tendency is already accelerating, thanks to the ease with which we can download new programs.

Since the beginning of the desktop computer revolution, we have bought our software in a box at the local software store or ordered it through a catalog. The programs come on diskettes or on CD-ROMs, and we install them in our computers using a setup program. Once there, we run them at will as local applications. WordPerfect, Excel, or Approach run on our machines and reside physically on our own hard disks. To update them, we go out and buy the latest version. But as I suggested earlier, aggressive commercialism will see an unprecedented wave of software development, with updates and revisions becoming available on the Net.

Rather than conceiving of the Internet as a remote place—"out there"—we begin to think of it as a kind of virtual hard disk, a disk that yields up information and programs as required, but only mimics the action of a physical hard disk. The growing ubiquity of the Net thus points to a future where what happens on its digital byways is more significant than what happens on our own machines. If the Internet begins to define not only how we conduct our research but also how we retrieve and run our software, then a browser is the background against which we will perform even the most mundane task, whether connected to the Net at the time or not. The Internet becomes the operating system, which is precisely what Microsoft has in mind as it shapes its Internet Explorer browser for merger with the Windows 95 desktop.

Folding the two environments together creates a significant issue as we look toward evaluating content and using the tools of knowledge assembly. These core competencies presuppose a rhetorical distance between the thing created on our own machine and the thing accessed or researched on a remote machine on the Internet. We have learned to apply critical standards to Web content, studying it in terms of its links to confirming data and its recency and authorship. The fusion of local content with Web-based information makes it even easier to fold bogus material into our work, and accentuates the need to weigh what we find against other sources, both on and off the Internet. For tighter links to the Net mean that more and more unfiltered, unedited material will be finding its way from hard disks to cyberspace and back again.

The Internet Toaster Pops

Distributing the operating system changes the shape of computing. And it raises conceptual questions about how we mine these resources. What kind of box do we use to connect to the Internet and to display the diverse media we'd like to bring into the home and office? In today's world, the difference between delivery mechanisms couldn't be greater. A television costs $100 and up; a computer, equipped with an adequate selection of the multimedia tools needed for the Internet, runs $1,700 to $2,000 or more. Yet the price differential, huge as it is, separates technologies that have begun to converge. Does a network-ready computer have to cost so much?

Perhaps not. If we accept the idea that the Internet is becoming a computing platform, then it's a short step to reconsidering the status of the desktop computer itself. Companies like Sun, Oracle, and IBM are questioning whether a different kind of box wouldn't make more sense. One that housed fewer hardware resources but interfaced so seamlessly with the Net that cyberspace would be an extension of the machine's user interface. Thus Oracle's vision: a $500 device that contains a keyboard, screen, and microprocessor, but no disk drives. Let the Internet store your resources, and use Java-based applications as your primary software tools.

Because its chief source of content as well as power is the Internet itself, the machine stays up to date. Acknowledging that the network is the user's source of information, the network box doesn't need a state-of-the-art processor as much as a seamless connection; it relies on the transmission and delivery of network data packets, which are dependent upon macro-issues like bandwidth and telecommunications infrastructure rather than the purchasing decisions of a buyer. The price is low, and the model is closer to that of the VCR or television set than to the desktop computer, thus corresponding to the needs of the average user rather than the technophile.

The terminology for these devices is likewise democratic. They're referred to as *Internet appliances*, or even *Internet toasters,* to link them in our minds with the tools we keep around the house, and thus to demystify the experience of using them. With the Net as your hard disk, storage space no longer determines which programs you can run or how much data you can store. For that matter, a network computer like this, simple in its workings and easy to configure, changes the one-to-one relationship between user and machine. Many a frustrated user will attest to the appeal of a machine that needn't be constantly tweaked to eke out the best performance, or serviced for the odd glitches that are the consequence of its complexity.

If we presuppose two categories of Internet machines, a regular personal computer and a specialized Internet appliance, then we re-create in some ways the distinction between computer and television that exists today. The Internet toaster is cheap and makes few demands; the computer is expensive and requires expertise. Both point to a convergence between differing types of content delivery, yet the one keeps processor power in the hands of the desktop user, while the other puts it in the care of the network. The Internet toaster is readily replaced if it becomes obsolete, although its reliance upon the Net lengthens the upgrade cycle considerably; after all, changes to the system in this case mean changes and revisions to its downloadable software.

But the case for the Internet toaster is laden with controversy. For the device harkens back to an earlier model of computing, one that seemed to have been superseded by the rise of the desktop machine. When mainframe computers ruled business and users could reach them only through terminals on their desktops, access to processor power in any form seemed wondrous. But today, familiar with managing their own processing power, users may find it difficult to revert to a terminal-based model. A business case can be made in terms of cost and upkeep, but individuals may balk at ceding control of their computing operations to a remote network.

And that is precisely what the Internet toaster sets out to do. It treats the network in the same light that terminals—display units with no real processing power—treated the mainframe computers they accessed. The consequence being that a remote network outage shuts down work on your machine, even as a slowdown caused by Net traffic slows operations on your desktop. To the extent to which power is removed from the individual, the question likewise becomes political. Computers are the great libertarian device of our time; they allow individuals to accomplish tasks that might otherwise be impossible to attempt. When power is transferred away from the machine to the network, the question becomes, who is in charge of the network? At present, the answer is, in essence, nobody. But the Internet toaster forces us to ask whether this will always be true. Can we foresee a future in which government control over the network shuts down options for individuals without local computing power? And do we want to gamble on the shape of government in 10 years? In 20?

Compaq Computer's CEO Eckhard Pfeiffer sees computers in the low-end Internet appliance price range in the near future; his company is working on $500 machines that will be Internet-ready. But the proposed Compaq box is more than an appliance;

with its 8MB of RAM; it's to be an inexpensive, though connectable, computer, rather than a terminal. Compaq calls these devices "disposable PCs," under the apparent assumption that consumers consider $500 electronic gadgets as discardable as used milk containers. But if the term is unfortunate, the idea is powerful. If we do arrive at a $500 network device, it will be because the cost of manufacturing computer components has dropped low enough to allow full-featured computers to be sold at these levels. Standardization around cheap boxes seems a dead certainty.

Convergence and Divergence on the Web

Picture this: Your computer is capable of displaying hundreds of thousands of individual video stations, each of them with the ability to link seamlessly to other sites through a diverse range of media types, and each with built-in interactive capacity to allow you to communicate with its creators or to participate in its ongoing discussions. This World Wide Web—the true broadband heir to today's nascent technology—is less fanciful than you may think. Cheaper access makes the Internet ubiquitous, with intriguing implications for how we view it in relation to traditional media. In the early chapters, I pointed out that the Internet as a demand medium contrasts with broadcast media like television and even print (in the sense that print is created for a mass audience and distributed accordingly, even as television is broadcast to the population at large). But what happens to this distinction if we bring to the Web page the full-blown multimedia experience of live video, coupled with the

Net's native interactivity? The answer is that we conflate the two worlds in powerful ways. What we ultimately create is a form of switchable, enhanced, and highly democratized television.

Driving the change will be vast increases in bandwidth—the capacity of the network to carry data. In a report studying how the Internet's data pipes will expand between now and the year 2005,[2] Sun Microsystems sees three waves of Internet bandwidth, with a heavy emphasis on video. The first wave involves the continued use of existing telephone networks running at rates up to 28 Kbps, the speed of the fastest modem connection now available. This is essentially today's network infrastructure as people upgrade to faster modems, adequate for text and the transmission of Web pages with still images, but becoming overloaded by increased use of audio and moving video, especially since these events coincide with the continued growth of the network among first-time users.

Thus the second phase, which the Sun report predicts will begin sometime in 1997 and will involve Integrated Services Digital Networking, or ISDN, technology. ISDN provides roughly four times the capacity of a conventional telephone line at roughly twice the price; the user winds up with workable moving video, albeit at relatively slow rates, and reliable connections at faster speeds than before. But ISDN itself is considered a stopgap measure, leading up to the third wave, which will begin in 1998 and will feature broadband network capabilities with speeds in the area of 2 megabits per second. At these speeds, broadcast-quality moving video is now a reality; in fact, 2Mbps is a speed higher than today's T-1 connection, used by many businesses to create access to the Internet for entire offices full of connected computers. Early implementations of this broadband capacity may involve high bandwidth from provider to customer and slower speeds on the return leg, but the report sees broadband moving video in both directions as a standard by the year 2002.

By 2005, opine the authors, 197 million sites will be connected; we can only speculate on how many active pages of information (if the page metaphor remains valid then) will be in place. In this world, the Internet experience will have the immediacy of a CNN live report and the interactivity of a telephone, all supplemented with the digital tools we've seen in action on the World Wide Web. Just as today's Web allows anyone to become a publisher of content, so tomorrow's Internet will allow anyone to become a video producer, with inevitable consequences in terms of quality. We will be able to craft by 2005 entire Web video stations around individual subjects with scalpel-like precision. Further developments in Internet audio will likewise allow communities of users to set up sound or video teleconferencing from the desktop, a tool that will change the dynamics of corporate travel just as it changes the experience of the individual user, connecting to a video discussion group, online class, or chat channel from home.

The idea of the "pointcast"—specific content tailored for the individual user and distributed through the network—is thus taken to its logical conclusion: an Internet with no discernible degradation in image quality from other forms of content delivery, and hence a network that puts the power of today's broadcast technology in the hands of the amateur, just as desktop publishing software puts the creation of newsletters, brochures, and reports in the hands of anyone with a computer and laser printer. The rhetoric of hypermedia we examined earlier is extended to the individual video studio and its live Web channel. Key questions will still be: What am I seeing, and what is being ignored? To what other resources does this content point, and how representative are they? How can I balance the viewpoint I'm seeing with dissenting information?

And what of television itself? Will today's broadcast model disappear, overcome by the rise of the computer networks? The answer is emphatically no. We count on the work of our information filters—editors, producers, directors, marketers—to make our movies, to develop our television series, to gather the work of our writers, and present these to us in easily accessible form. Television, then, will continue its parallel development, perhaps through hybrid devices that connect either to the Internet or to the broadcast networks, or through a separate technology that maximizes the benefits of both. For just as the ability of the individual to publish an on-line newsletter has not undermined the creation of *The New York Times*, the distribution of video tools and programming on the Net will not threaten the major content providers.

The Internet as Experience

Combining high bandwidth with video and audio capabilities, we can turn the Internet experience sharply in the direction of simile and metaphor. Virtual reality reshapes the Internet interface by representing visually what once had to be described in words or graphics, and by allowing actions to be mediated by mouse movements rather than command entries. Craft such a digital world and you can translate a concrete act into a symbol, then manipulate the symbol to help people visualize complex procedures.

A virtual world is an interface of unique power; it translates a complicated computer task into the universe of objects and motion we all inhabit. Despite the best efforts of programmers, however, virtual reality (VR) is still an experiment, particularly on the Internet, where groundbreaking sites like Worlds Chat are exploring ways to bring people together on screens that at least model a physical space. But if virtual reality allows a programmer to set up the experience of using the Internet as an environment, we can see environment-building as the Net's future. Perhaps I run a bookstore. I could set up an Internet site using virtual reality software that would suggest to the user that he or she were entering a physical place. I could create, instead of a menu of possible actions, a graphical interior complete with rows of shelves, a front desk for orders and payment, a catalog for finding titles, and perhaps a nook filled with armchairs where people could stop to chat with other bibliophiles who might wander in.

The advantage of this environment is that it's both memorable and easy to use. It creates such clear parallels between using the bookstore on computer and walking into its real-world analogue that any user, no matter how poorly versed in using computers or the Internet itself, can navigate it successfully. Developers talk of creating virtual worlds around databases, for example, in which users access collections of information through an on-screen library simulacrum. A Web site could display different document collections as buildings, each with its own style or color.

Virtual reality's implications for similar modeling in business and educational settings seem enormous, for it allows us to model complex systems, move within them to observe their functions, and experiment in provocative ways with their features. Corporate or educational training environments can be built that offer, like a good flight simulator, the ability to model situations and replay them at little cost. Imagine a virtual nuclear reactor, a virtual Jupiter, a virtual galaxy, and ponder the advantages of being able to enter and move about in each with three-dimensional verisimilitude.

We refer to virtual reality applications as three-dimensional because they allow us to operate in an imagined space through all three axes of height, length, and depth. On a conventional screen display, I would choose icons on which to click, moving the cursor up or down or sideways as necessary. What I can't do is reach behind an object or navigate around it. In the virtual reality world, I can use the mouse to simulate motion into a scene, thus mimicking the experience of walking through a landscape or a building. I can go through a door, up a flight of stairs, behind a statue, as needed.

Networked VR is interpreted by Web browsers, which means they must have at their disposal a robust language that allows them to render this complicated information in an aesthetically pleasing as well as useful way. Driven by research at companies like Silicon Graphics, InterVista Software, and Template Graphics Software, Virtual Reality Modeling Language, or VRML (usually pronounced "vermal"), is being developed by a committee that is examining various standards options. It may one day offer a replacement, although more likely a supplement, to the Web's HTML, with its support for the kind of interactive video and audio experience that virtual reality demands.

The integration between virtual reality and browser is of necessity tight. InterVista, for example, has released a product called Worldview 3-D, a Web browser designed specifically for the virtual reality environment. The product can be used in stand-alone fashion, or it can function as an add-on to conventional browsers like Mosaic or Netscape; indeed, Microsoft has licensed Worldview 3-D for its Internet Explorer browser, which will thus launch the Inter-Vista product whenever it encounters Web pages written in VRML format. And products supporting 3-D applications at the server level have begun to appear. Paramount International's Virtual Home Space Builder, for example, allows users to create virtual environments by dragging and dropping icons. Such tools will increasingly be integrated into our Net software.

The most compelling aspect of virtual reality is that it may inspire new forms of community-building. Earlier, I explained how VR could be used to build a chat space in which people see others represented on the screen as avatars and move about in an eerie cyberspace world to explore and socialize. The success of Worlds Chat is mirrored by Worlds Incorporation's AlphaWorld (http://www.worlds.net/), which picks up on the idea of avatars and imagined environments to add a range of user capabilities. You can set up a shop on AlphaWorld or purchase a tract of "land." Users type their words in bubbles of text, something like the captions that show a character's speech in a comic book. But it's not difficult to imagine live audio moving into this scenario, given the rapid development of voice applications carried by the network. And we've seen that in a world of widening bandwidth, live video is but a matter of time.

If you think of AlphaWorld as a virtual community, it will be obvious that, like most modern communities, it is destined to grow. Users can build structures within the AlphaWorld virtual space or open stores; they can, in fact, engage in many of the same activities, or the virtual equivalent of them, that they pursue in real life. The virtual community, then, begins to take on the shape of the physical world, a metaphor in phosphor that mirrors typical social interactions. Seen in the light of the virtual community, the Internet can become a fascinating attempt to re-create the universe. I move through a virtual city and bump into someone's avatar on the sidewalk. What happens? Should the software let me pass through the ghostly apparition like some sort of spiritual entity? Or should it model the laws of physics as we understand them, so that I bounce off the avatar? If so, we must teach the virtual world something more about physics, thus learning more ourselves. If I step off the edge of a virtual building, do I fall? What sort of rules do we build into virtual worlds that we may not enjoy in the physical world, and which rules must we carry over for the simulation to be effective?

These are not questions for the faint of heart, for they tug at the purposes for which we are developing virtual reality. By modeling worlds, we will invariably learn more about our own, with the likely eventuality that a virtual world will, in its own way, prove as surprising and multitextured as a physical one. And it's just possible that extended and highly developed virtual environments may offer us clues as we attempt to master the critical issues of living together in a physical world that is running out of resources and facing shortages in key areas of skill and education.

The virtual world is therefore something more than an interface. Unlike HTML, which was developed to display information in standardized formats, VRML points to a sharpened sense of user participation because it allows people to meet each other in customized visual spaces they recognize. The creative aspects of offering virtual worlds that can be defined and extended by their participants mean that the Internet of tomorrow will continue to sport gamelike features that encourage exploration and risk taking. A modeled environment, unlike a real one, can be tweaked just to see what happens; failed experiments can be discarded, successes expanded.

But despite the fact that Worlds Incorporation has signed agreements with companies like Sony, Mitsubishi, and VISA International to infuse its technology into their on-line efforts, the notion that virtual reality will become the standard Internet interface is problematic. The typical business transaction, like the typical search through a library, is more efficiently managed without the surrounding envelope of virtual scenery. Faced with a choice, I will enter keywords in a search engine rather than choose to navigate through a cityscape or a graphical search desk to do repetitive work. Where virtual reality is likely to excel is in the communications arena, people to people, and in the development of interactive simulation and games. These are fundamentally different activities, and they demand interfaces like those buildable through VRML.

Which makes it more, not less, likely that we will continue to have multiple interface standards for the Internet, each maximized to display the data needed in its own pursuit. Need to talk to a distant colleague? A virtual world armed with live audio and video makes for a quick transatlantic conference, tailored to your personality; numerous companies will set about tailoring such interfaces for customers to come. Want to be absorbed by an alternate reality? A virtual re-creation of nineteenth-century Africa, Mars, or the streets of Los Angeles puts you into the game and lets you take on all challengers from the comfort of your living room. But when you need to check an annual report or run a search for Web pages on chemistry, the virtual world yields to the straight-up world of forms and text. Multipurpose browsers, capable of handling all these display chores, should remain the tool of choice for years to come.

Mastering an Internet containing thousands of virtual worlds forces us to draw upon all our skills of content evaluation and hypertextual navigation. The rhetoric of the virtual world is inclusive, dependent upon the skills of its designer. We must understand its metaphor and be able to evaluate its connection with the underlying reality it represents before we can draw meaningfully on its content. If VR programmers are world builders, we end users will have to learn to be the critics of worlds, giving us an amusingly godlike perspective on the digital universe. For a virtual world makes us ask not only if a given fact is true, but also if its symbol is appropriate or realistic. A simulation is only as good as its modeling. And while the question we must ask with hypertext is, what links are being left out, the question we must ask of a virtual world is, how does its shape serve the interests of its creator?

Implications of Internet Change

As the Internet becomes more broadly established and provides enhanced display and navigational features, sociological questions arise. What does it mean when we can use hyperlinks to connect to vast amounts of supporting information for any subject? The fact that we can do so is now incontestable, but does the act of access change the way we regard information? And what of the written word itself, evidently the beneficiary of this enlarged connectivity? Does the fact that a statement appears on a screen give it more or less weight than its counterpart on the printed page? How do we use it?

These philosophical questions point to real-world dilemmas. In his book *The Gutenberg Elegies*, Sven Birkerts ponders just what multimedia might mean for education: "We might question, too, whether there is not in learning as in physical science a principle of energy conservation. Does a gain in one area depend upon a loss in another? My guess would be that every lateral attainment is purchased with a sacrifice of depth. The student may, through a program on Shakespeare, learn an immense amount about Elizabethan politics, the construction of the Globe theater, the origins of certain plays in the writings of Plutarch, the etymology of key terms, and so on, but will this dazzled student find the concentration, the will, to live with the often burred and prickly language of the plays themselves? The play's the thing—but will it be? Wouldn't the sustained exposure to a souped-up cognitive collage not begin to affect the attention span, the ability if not willingness to sit with one text for extended periods, butting up against its cruxes, trying to excavate meaning from the original rhythms and syntax? The gurus of interaction love to say that the student learns best by doing, but let's not forget that reading a work is also a kind of doing."[3]

Thus we run up against a paradox of knowledge: Birkerts seems to be saying that there can be too much of a good thing. No one would contest that our ability to retrieve at will from the information horde is an advantage, but if it comes with a corresponding diminution in our ability to think cognitively, then the Internet could be seen as a subversive agent, undermining our educational values at a time when they are already overwhelmed by lowered standards and disruptive influences, from television to video games. The danger of packaging information in too cohesive a format, as in a multimedia CD-ROM, is that it performs the necessary legwork for the student or researcher; part of the learning process, and some would argue, the most important part, happens in the act of acquiring the needed information. Doing teaches.

Unfortunately for the theorists of decline, however, the causal relationship between technology and educational crisis has yet to be established. If it makes sense on an intuitive level that time spent in front of a computer—or a television—is time away from homework or other kinds of learning, then it also makes sense that several decades of social engineering and educational experimentation may have played a significant role in causing the present impasse. To what, then, do we turn?

We can hope that the Internet and related technologies may force the development of alternative educational strategies to supplement our current failed policies. Ironically, a combination of nineteenth-century educational discipline and twenty-first-century technological tools could be the catalyst for rebirth, allowing the exchange of ideas at fiber-optic speeds, driving development of a generation of generalists who refute the awkward pigeonholing of the specialist, and who can explore career change and personal growth from anyplace they can locate a telephone jack or Net hookup. The notion that access to multimedia supplementary materials undermines the close reading of texts doesn't take into account the number of people who might be drawn to those texts precisely because of the availability and persuasiveness of such materials. Nor does it recognize those newly enfranchised to learn by a technology that offers them networked access to hitherto unavailable collections of information.

What of the concerns about Internet content, particularly with regard to privacy and pornography? My premise throughout has been that technology can resolve the problems it creates. If a government cannot eliminate pornography at the local newsstand, it cannot eliminate it when it crosses borders at light speed through a decentralized network. But the same technological milieu that can distribute dubious photographs by digital means can also produce software solutions that allow people to block offending sites from their machines, or take advantage of newly developed rating systems for Web content. Rather than censorship, we need to make it possible for parents to control the content that appears on home PCs. Early programs like SurfWatch and NetNanny already point in this direction, and public demand will nourish a market for other developers who find solutions to this problem. The same is true of software to block information in private databases from prying eyes on the Net.

It's clear that the Internet's very connectivity is what disturbs us, not so much because it reflects an intrusion of technology into our lives, but because it puts us in closer contact with each other, for all the good and bad that entails. A newsgroup can serve as a focused meeting place for like-minded people who otherwise would never have been aware of each other's existence. It can also become a refuge for splinter groups and extremists, whose ability to find others who share their views only confirms their belief that their views are tenable. A newsgroup of pedophiles validates pedophilia to those who frequent it; there, at least, their ideas go unchallenged.

This ability to create self-supporting clusters of experience becomes threatening only when it takes place without a sense of context. The message of digital literacy is that no fact should be allowed to stand in isolation; we proceed by building a cache of verified content to reach conclusions. The verified statement branches out along the threads of hypertext to be confirmed by statements at other computer sites; it operates within a structure of validation and cross-referencing on which we have learned to rely. The Internet becomes dangerous only when these principles are ignored. Sites that do so, closing out alternative viewpoints, offering little or no attribution, focusing their links internally for purposes of propaganda rather than out to the broader Net, should now be readily identifiable. We can defeat their provincialism by understanding how they function and insisting on sound standards of reliability.

If there is one thing we can assume, it's that technology will not vanish because some of us raise questions about its impact on society. And the Internet seems destined to become just as significant a player in the way we shop for and buy goods and services as it does in the way we conduct an education. This is true despite the fact that human nature still insists upon the company of others; if the physical marketplace will not vanish, it's clearly going to be supplemented with the on-line store. Fast delivery, searchable catalogs, and convenience are powerful incentives to shop on the machine.

A commercialized Internet is one that needs watching to ensure that the social values we want this network to enhance for education, the arts, and the public good aren't lost in the so-called tragedy of the commons. This phenomenon, the dividing up of public spaces by business until eventually none are left, was first identified by Garrett Hardin in a 1968 article in *Science* magazine.[4] While finding a free-market solution to the dilemma of public spaces is beyond the purview of this book, the Net's commercialization is irreversible. Technology driven by capitalism fires the Internet's engines, and will account for faster development in the next five years than networking has seen in its history. The only way to adapt to its demands is to use the tools of digital literacy to examine content with a mind honed on rationality and skepticism.

Notes

Chapter 1

1. Trish Information Services conducted this survey for publisher O'Reilly & Associates in 1995; the numbers were somewhat controversial because it had become commonplace in that year to cite some 15 million Internet users in the United States.
2. This survey was conducted by Wirthlin Worldwide; it finds that 27 million people in the U.S. are 'consistent users.' Its numbers are almost certainly inflated.
3. Numerous other estimates exist. Forrester Research sees 24 million U.S. users, while International Data Corporation points to a whopping 56 million users worldwide. For some time to come, we'll have to take each growth estimate with a grain of salt, bearing in mind the different methods each company uses to come to its conclusions.
4. The 100 percent figure is from market research firm FIND/SVP. Estimates of Internet growth rates are frequently as exaggerated as guesses about its size, but the 100 percent figure is supportable.
5. This is Durlacher Multimedia; its estimates are on the high side, but most studies suggest between 120 million and 200 million by the early years of the twenty-first

century. This, of course, assumes that current growth rates are not interrupted.

6. George Gilder made this point in an article, "Auguring the Matrix," by Jeff Ubois, in *Internet World*, November, 1995.

7. Durlacher Multimedia, for example, finds median income in the United Kingdom about half of what O'Reilly's report finds for U.S. users. A study by the Graphics, Visualization and Usability Center at the Georgia Institute of Technology sees fewer women on the Internet than the O'Reilly study.

8. This material is from the Georgia Institute of Technology Study, which is the most complete analysis of Internet demographics yet attempted.

9. Postman, Neil, from "Informing Ourselves to Death," a speech presented to a meeting of the German Informatics Society (Gesellschaft für Informatik) in Stuttgart on October 11, 1990. Also see Postman's *Technopoly: The Surrender of Culture to Technology* (New York: Vintage Books, 1993).

10. Ibid. Also see Postman's *Technopoly: The Surrender of Culture to Technology* (New York: Vintage Books, 1993).

11. As told to Howard Rheingold in his book *The Virtual Community* (New York: Addison-Wesley, 1993), pp. 228–229.

12. The Nielsen study was released at the 1995 Internet World trade show in Boston. It was based on 4,200 random telephone calls and some 32,000 questionnaires filled out on the World Wide Web. Nielsen cites its margin of error at plus or minus 4 percent.

13. Birkerts, Sven, *The Gutenberg Elegies: The Fate of Reading in an Electronic Age* (Boston: Faber and Faber, 1994), p. 156.

14. To be fair, the reaction of academics to the networking revolution has been more diverse than these remarks may suggest. One of the most important works in this area is Richard Lanham's *The Electronic Word: Democracy, Technology and the Arts* (Chicago: University of Chicago Press, 1993). A sample: "All of these machina-

tions upon greatness are pedagogical techniques that open literary texts to people whose talents are not intrinsically 'literary,' people who want, in all kinds of intuitive ways, to operate upon experience rather than passively receive it. Codex books limit the wisdom of the Great Books to students who are Great Readers—as, to be sure, all of us who debate curricular matters were and are. Electronic text blows that limitation wide open. It offers new ways to democratize the arts, ways of the sort society is asking us to provide. If groups of people newly come to the world of liberal learning cannot unpack the Silenus box of wisdom with the tools they bring, maybe we can redesign the box electronically, so that the tools they have, the talents they already possess, will suffice. We need not necessarily compromise the wisdom therein." Lanham sees the personal computer as essentially a rhetorical device and, later, "the ultimate postmodern work of art." For more on this debate, see Myron Tuman's *Word Perfect: Literacy in the Computer Age* (Pittsburgh: Pittsburg University Press, 1992); also Jay David Bolter, *Writing Space: The Computer, Hypertext, and the History of Writing* (Hillsdale, N.J.: Lawrence Erlbaum, 1991).

15. Stoll, Clifford, *The Cuckoo's Egg* (New York: Doubleday, 1989).

16. Stoll, Clifford, *Silicon Snake Oil: Second Thoughts on the Information Highway.* (New York: Doubleday, 1995), p. 58.

17. Frisch, Max, *Homo Faber* (San Diego: Harcourt Brace, 1994).

18. Sale's *The Conquest of Paradise* (New York: Alfred A. Knopf, 1990) is a lament for what might have been had the Europeans powers never discovered North America, with a vision of reality not dissimilar from Rousseau's in the eighteenth century; he later moved on to examine the Luddites, of whom he considers himself a modern-day descendant, in *Rebels against the Future: The Luddites and Their War on the Industrial Revolution* (New York: Addison-Wesley, 1995). Bill

McKibben's *The End of Nature* (New York: Random House, 1989) discusses how human activities have changed the natural order with possibly disastrous consequences.

Chapter 2

1. Ancient papyrus rolls could hold no more than a thousand or so lines of text, meaning that a long book would have to be divided into multiple rolls—thus the 24 "books" that make up the *Odyssey*. Imagine trying to work your way through 24 rolls of papyrus as you looked for a favorite passage. For more on ancient manuscripts, see James O'Donnell's "St. Augustine to NREN: The Tree of Knowledge and How It Grows," which can be found on-line at http://ccat.sas.upenn.edu/jod/nasig.html. This paper was originally published in *The Serials Librarian* 23.3/4 (1993), 21–41.
2. These figures are from Neil Postman, op. cit.
3. I owe special thanks to William Graves, director of the Institute for Academic Technology, for sharing this metaphor with me; Graves has explored it in several published articles on the future of educational computing.
4. Dawkins, Richard, *The Selfish Gene* (Oxford: Oxford University Press, 1976).
5. This is actually a rather limited definition if examined historically. For most of the history of the English language, literacy referred to the state of being well educated, particularly in terms of literature. The word comes originally from the Latin word *litteratus*, derived from *littera*, meaning letter; a literate person in this sense was lettered.
6. Sherry Turkle's *Life on the Screen* is a psychologist's look at the way networked computers allow us to take on different identities, and thus explore aspects of ourselves

that would otherwise remain hidden. We're probably at the beginning of a wave of such studies as we explore how computers are changing social relationships.

7. C. S. Doyle's study "Information Literacy in an Information Society: A Concept for the Information Age" (Syracuse, N.Y.: ERIC Clearinghouse on Information & Technology (IR-97) examines many of these issues; it is one of the few studies to do so, though I also recommend Bill Tally's "The New Literacy of the Net: Judging the Quality of Information in an Unfiltered Medium" (Electronic Learning, Sept. 1995, v. 15, n. 1, p. 14). Given the dimensions of the paradigm shift, it is remarkable that so little attention has thus far been paid to its implications.

8. For more on the topic of literacy in the electronic era, see Trish Ridgeway's "Information Literacy: An Introductory Reading List" (*College and Research Libraries News*, July/Aug. 1990, p. 645); equally informative, and more provocative, is Stephen Foster's "Information Literacy: Some Misgivings" (*American Libraries*, April 1, 1993, v. 24, p. 344). Finally, see Michael and Rhona Hauben's "Netizens: On the History and Impact of Usenet and the Internet," which is published on-line and is available through the following URL: http://www.columbia.edu/~hauben/netbook/.

9. In his book *The Micro Revolution Revisited* (New Jersey: Rowan and Allenheld Co., 1984), p. 35.

Chapter 3

1. Stephenson, Neal, *Snow Crash* (Bantam Books, 1992), pp. 26–27. The so-called cyberpunk school of science fiction has been largely toothless, in my view, since so many authors did little more than superimpose today's technology on a hypothetical future. Stephenson, though, is another thing entirely, one of the most provocative writers working the frontier between technology and litera-

ture we have. When Stephenson writes about the future, it *feels* like the future.

2. The IBM software I was evaluating that day is called TeamFocus; it's a workgroup-based conferencing system that allows meetings to take place in the same physical space, with participants using computers to hammer out consensus in a variety of ways, answering questions and examining other people's responses to the issues. TeamFocus and a much more familiar IBM product, Lotus Notes, both send the message that computer networking can be a potent way to get people talking who otherwise would remain silent.

Chapter 4

1. As reported by Tracy Thompson in *The Washington Post* and reprinted in *The News & Observer* (Raleigh, N.C.), February 26, 1996.

2. You can find this story recounted in some detail in Risks Digest 15.57, where Dan Yurman posted it. Risks is itself a mailing list that deals with computer problems and their solutions, many of them societal in nature.

3. The story was reported in the *Houston Chronicle* on February 14, 1996, and later distributed through the EDUPAGE mailing list, which carries network news and related technology developments. This is a classic case of the Internet itself being used to correct errors it had been responsible for creating.

Chapter 5

1. Austin Meredith compares conventional research to a project known as the Stack of the Artist of Kouroo, after

a reference by Henry David Thoreau. This project attempts to build a massive hypermedia database around the works of Thoreau as a test bed for what can be accomplished in fusing computer research with the humanities. Some 19 million hypertext links have already been created, including biographies of Thoreau's acquaintances, works written in and around Concord during his lifetime, a master chronology of Thoreau's life with over 4,500 screens, and much more. The dataset is obviously massive; what the computer provides is the ability to move through it as readily as we humans use a bound book.

2. A fascinating discussion of this topic took place in the History of Cyberspace mailing list in mid-1996. The entire list is archived at http://www.reach.com/matrix/community-memory.html.

3. See V. Balasubramanian's "State of the Art Review on Hypermedia Issues and Applications," available on-line at http://www.isg.sfu.ca/~duchier/misc/hypertext_review/index.html.

4. First published in the *Atlantic Monthly*, Bush's work can now be consulted on-line at http://www.csi.uottawa.ca/~dduchier/misc/vbush/as-we-may-think.html. Bush wrote about a device called a *mexex*, which performed many of the retrieval functions of today's computers.

5. An early and persistent voice in the hypertext debate is that of Theodor Holm Nelson, whose Xanadu project is an attempt to create a universal storehouse of human knowledge; it has also been described as "the longest-running vaporware project in the history of computing." But Nelson remains a fascinating figure, and is by many regarded as one of the fathers of hypertext. You can sample his work at http://www.mi.aau.dk/~cabo/Hypermedie_95_opg.2/nelson.html. This is an on-line version of Nelson's "Opening Hypertext: A Memoir," which appeared in *Literacy Online: The Promise (and Peril) of Reading and Writing with Computers*, edited by Myron C. Tuman (Pittsburgh: Univ. of Pittsburgh Press,

1992), pp. 43-57. The Xanadu home page is at http://www. xanadu.com.au/xanadu/.

Chapter 6

1. Fillmore's speech was printed in revised form in *On the Internet*, the journal of The Internet Society, in its September/October 1995 issue, p. 37 ff.
2. Ibid., p. 38.
3. Ibid., p. 41.
4. Bush's work remains provocative today; anyone concerned with the shape of the Internet should read it. Fortunately, the article is available on-line at http://www. csi.uottawa.ca/~dduchier/misc/vbush/as-we-may-think. html. One can only wonder at what Bush's reaction would have been to see his prediction so tangibly validated in the form of the article that first advanced these ideas.
5. Few cases of copyright infringement on the Internet have been decided by the courts, but lobbyists from the music, film, and software industries have demanded that Congress rewrite copyright laws to reflect the changes created by the Internet. In one case, a former minister of the Church of Scientology has been taken to court for posting church documents without the church's permission. In another, the On-line Guitar Archive, an FTP site containing music for thousands of songs, was forced to cease operations when threatened with copyright infringement by EMI Music Publishing. A rewritten copyright law poses many questions, not the least among which is this: Would Internet access providers be compelled to monitor on-line content and be held responsible for violations? The effects of such a ruling could be devastating to the access business, imposing an obligation many would find impossible to meet.

6. This challenge, of course, extends to the three other forms of intellectual property—patents, trademarks, and trade secrets—as well. All three will be in need of adjustment as computer law tackles cyberspace.

7. The Corporation for National Research Initiatives, for example, is working with funding from ARPA and the Library of Congress to construct a system called Electronic Copyright Management System, which encrypts materials distributed to on-line libraries. People interested in reading the work would buy a software key that would unlock it.

8. While copyright protection schemes of various kinds have appeared, at least one prominent Internet figure has argued for the elimination of copyright altogether. John Perry Barlow, a cofounder of the Electronic Frontier Foundation, questions whether the idea of intellectual property is valid in the digital environment. Barlow's provocative views are unlikely to find supporters among content publishers.

9. "Such an approach," writes Fillmore, "using the value-added external links and the readers' attention to which they appeal as the two poles of commerce in the online publishing experiment, constitutes a working hierarchy which should preserve free, or relatively free, access to thought and ideas. Assume . . . that the text files for the book, the ASCII files, would be freely available to any who wanted them. What would be of value, and what readers would pay for, would be the customized contextual referencing surrounding the text files, the value added. In short, such a hierarchy preserves the free public library component of paper publishing with the free availability of ASCII, while capitalizing on the unique properties of the Net by making possible a kinetic core of content, linked into distributive online context with a protean set of links, customized for individual uses or groups of users." From "A Reader's Attention: Catching that Rare and Migratory Bird Online," a speech delivered at the AIC Conference in London, January 24,

1995, and available online at http://www.obs-us.com/obs/english/papers/bird.htm.

Chapter 7

1. "Search for Past Life on Mars: Possible Relic Biogenic Activity in Martian Meteorite ALH84001" by David S. McKay, Everett K. Gibson Jr., Kathie L. Thomas-Keprta, Hojatollah Vali, Christopher S. Romanek, Simon J. Clemett, Xavier D. F. Chillier, Claude R. Maechling, and Richard N. Zare, *Science*, August 16, 1996. The full text of the article is available on-line at http://www.eurekalert.org/E-lert/current/public_releases/mars/924/924.html.
2. Howard Rheingold, whose on-line book was discussed earlier, is perhaps the strongest proponent of this idea. He has created a site called Electric Minds (http://www.minds.com/) to explore the combination of electronic publishing and live conferencing.
3. "Similar UNM Meteorite Study Found No Evidence of Life," from the *Albuquerque Journal*, August 8, 1996.

Chapter 8

1. Gilder, George, *Life After Television* (New York: WW Norton & Co., 1994), p. 79.
2. The report, by John Moroney and John Matthews, appeared in *SunWorld*, the company's electronic magazine, in Vol. 9, No. 12, Dec. 1995. The study was conducted by a research firm called Ovum Limited, based in London.
3. Birkerts, Sven, *The Gutenberg Elegies: The Fate of Reading in an Electronic Age* (Boston: Faber and Faber, 1994).
4. Hardin, Garrett, "The Tragedy of the Commons," *Science* 162 (1968), pp. 1243–1248.

Index